The Communist Hypothesis

The Communist Hypothesis

ALAIN BADIOU

Translated by
David Macey and Steve Corcoran

VERSO
London • New York

First published in English by Verso 2010
© Verso 2010
Translation David Macey and Steve Corcoran © 2010
'A Brief Chronolgy of the Cultural Revolution'
translated by Bruno Bosted 2010
First published as *L'hypothése communiste*
Appendix first published as *Presentation de Mao, De la pratique et de la
contradiction, avec une lettre d'Alain Badiou et la réponse de Slavoj Žižek*
© La Fabrique 2008

The moral rights of the author and translator have been asserted

1 3 5 7 9 10 8 6 4 2

Verso
UK: 6 Meard Street, London W1F 0EG
USA: 20 Jay Street, Suite 1010, Brooklyn, NY 11201
www.versobooks.com

Verso is the imprint of New Left Books

ISBN-13: 978-1-84467-600-2

British Library Cataloguing in Publication Data
A catalogue record for this book is available from the British Library

Library of Congress Cataloging-in-Publication Data
A catalog record for this book is available from the Library of Congress

Typeset by Hewer Text UK Ltd, Edinburgh
Printed in the USA by Maple Vail

Contents

Preamble: What Is Called Failure?

1

The mid-1970s saw the beginnings of the ebb the 'red decade' ushered in by the fourfold circumstances of national liberation struggles (in Vietnam and Palestine in particular), the worldwide student and youth movement (Germany, Japan, the USA, Mexico . . .), factory revolts (France and Italy) and the Cultural Revolution in China. It finds its subjective form in a resigned surrender, in a return to customs – including electoral customs – deference towards the capitalo-parliamentarian or 'Western' order, and the conviction that to want something better is to want something worse. It finds its intellectual form in what, in France, acquired the very strange name of 'the new philosophy'. Despite the change of name, we have here, almost unchanged, all the arguments of the American anti-communism of the

1950s: socialist regimes are loathsome despotisms and bloody dictatorships. At the level of the state, this socialist 'totalitarianism' must be contrasted with representative democracy which, while it is of course imperfect, is by far the least bad form of government. At the moral level, which is the most important in philosophical terms, we must preach the values of the 'free world' centred on and protected by the United States. Because it has ended in failure all over the world, the communist hypothesis is a criminal utopia that must give way to a culture of 'human rights', which combines the cult of freedom (including, of course, freedom of enterprise, the freedom to own property and to grow rich that is the material guarantee of all other freedoms) and a representation in which Good is a victim. Good is never anything more than the struggle against Evil, which is tantamount to saying that we must care only for those who present themselves, or who are exhibited, as the victims of Evil. As for Evil, it is everything that the free West designates as such, what Reagan called 'the Evil Empire'. Which brings us back to our starting point: the communist Idea, and so on.

For various reasons, this propaganda machine

is now obsolete, mainly because there is no longer a
single powerful state claiming to be communist, or even
socialist. Many rhetorical devices have of course been
recycled in the 'war against terror' which, in France, has
taken on the guise of an anti-Islamist crusade. And yet
no one can seriously believe that a particularist religious
ideology that is backward-looking in terms of its social
vision, and fascistic in both its conception of action
and its outcome, can replace a promise of universal
emancipation supported by three centuries of critical,
international and secular philosophy that exploited the
resources of science and mobilized, at the very heart
of the industrial metropolises, the enthusiasm of both
workers and intellectuals. Lumping together Stalin
and Hitler was already a sign of extreme intellectual
poverty: the norm by which any collective undertaking
has to be judged is, it was argued, the number of deaths
it causes. If that were really the case, the huge colonial
genocides and massacres, the millions of deaths in the
civil and world wars through which our West forged its
might, should be enough to discredit, even in the eyes of
'philosophers' who extol their morality, the parliamentary
regimes of Europe and America. What would be left for
those who scribble about Rights? How could they go on

singing the praises of bourgeois democracy as the only form of relative Good and making pompous predictions about totalitarianism when they are standing on top of heaps of victims? Lumping together Hitler, Stalin and Bin Laden now looks like a black farce. It indicates that our democratic West is none too fussy about the nature of the historic fuel it uses to keep its propaganda machine running. It is true that, these days, it has other fish to fry. After two short decades of cynically unequal prosperity, it is in the grip of a truly historical crisis and has to fall back on its 'democratic' pretensions, as it appears to have been doing for some time, with the help of walls and barbed-wire fences to keep out foreigners, a corrupt and servile media, overcrowded prisons and iniquitous legislation. The problem is that it is less and less capable of corrupting its local clientele and buying off the ferocious foreign regimes of the Mubaraks and Musharrafs who are responsible for keeping watch on the flocks of the poor.

What remains of the labours of the 'new philosophers' who have been enlightening us – or, in other words, deadening our minds – for 30 years now? What really remains of the great ideological machinery of freedom, human rights, the West and its values?

It all comes down to a simple negative statement that is as bald as it is flat and as naked as the day it was born: socialisms, which were the communist Idea's only concrete forms, failed completely in the twentieth century. Even they have had to revert to capitalism and non-egalitarian dogma. That failure of the Idea leaves us with no choice, given the complex of the capitalist organization of production and the state parliamentary system. Like it or not, we have to consent to it for lack of choice. And that is why we now have to save the banks rather than confiscate them, hand out billions to the rich and give nothing to the poor, set nationals against workers of foreign origin whenever possible, and, in a word, keep tight controls on all forms of poverty in order to ensure the survival of the powerful. No choice, I tell you! As our ideologues admit, it is not as though relying on the greed of a few crooks and unbridled private property to run the state and the economy was the absolute Good. But it is the only possible way forward. In his anarchist vision, Stirner described man, or the personal agent of History, as 'the Ego and his own'. Nowadays, it is 'Property as ego'.

Which means that we have to think about the notion

of failure. What exactly do we mean by 'failure' when
we refer to a historical sequence that experimented
with one or another form of the communist hypothesis?
What exactly do we mean when we say that all the
socialist experiments that took place under the
sign of that hypothesis ended in 'failure'? Was it a
complete failure? By which I mean: does it require
us to abandon the hypothesis itself, and to renounce
the whole problem of emancipation? Or was it merely
a relative failure? Was it a failure because of the form
it took or the path it explored? Was it a failure that
simply proves that it was not the right way to resolve
the initial problem?

A comparison will shed light on my conviction.
Take a scientific problem, which may well take the
form of a hypothesis until such time as it is resolved.
It could be, for example, that 'Fermat's theorem' is
a hypothesis if we formulate it as: 'For $>n$, I assume
that the equation $x^n + y^n = z^n$ has no whole solutions
(solutions in which x, y and z are whole numbers).'
Countless attempts were made to prove this, from
Fermat, who formulated the hypothesis (and claimed
to have proved it, but that need not concern us here), to
Wiles, the English mathematician, who really did prove

it a few years ago. Many of those attempts became the starting point for mathematical developments of great import, even though they did not succeed in solving the problem itself. It was therefore vital not to abandon the hypothesis for the three hundred years during which it was impossible to prove it. The lessons of all the failures, and the process of examining them and their implications, were the lifeblood of mathematics. In that sense, failure is nothing more than the history of the proof of the hypothesis, provided that the hypothesis is not abandoned. As Mao puts it, the logic of imperialists and all reactionaries the world over is 'make trouble, fail, make trouble again', but the logic of the people is 'fight, fail, fail again, fight again . . . till their victory'.[1]

It will be argued here, via a detailed discussion of three examples (May '68, the Cultural Revolution and the Paris Commune), that the apparent, and sometimes bloody, failures of events closely bound up with the communist hypothesis were and are stages in

---

1   'Cast Away illusions, Prepare for Struggle', *Selected Works of Mao Tse-Tung*, Vol. IV, Foreign Languages Press, 1969, p. 248.

its history. At least for all those who are not blinded by
the propagandist use of the notion of failure. Meaning
all those who are still inspired by the communist
hypotheses in so far as they are political subjects,
and irrespective of whether or not they actually use
the word 'communism'. In politics, it is thoughts,
organizations and deeds that count. Proper nouns,
such as Robespierre, Marx and Lenin, are sometimes
used as referents. Common nouns (revolution,
proletariat, socialism . . .) are in themselves much
less capable of naming a real sequence in the politics
of emancipation, and their use is rapidly exposed to
an inflation that has no content. Adjectives (resistant,
revisionist, imperialist . . .) are usually used only for
propaganda. That is because universality, which is the
real attribute of any corpus of truths, will have nothing
to do with predicates. A real politics knows nothing of
identities, even the identity – so tenuous, so variable
– of 'communists'. It knows only fragments of the real,
and an Idea of the real is testimony to the fact that the
work of its truth is ongoing.

2

Between the middle and the end of the 'red years' I was speaking about earlier, I had several opportunities to reach a verdict on failure, on the positive meaning of defeats. A revolutionary defeat is in fact always divided into a negative part (deaths, imprisonments, betrayals, loss of strength, fragmentation), which is often very obvious at the time, and a positive part, which usually takes a long time to emerge (a tactical and strategic reckoning, a change of action-models, the invention of new forms of organization). Between 1972 and 1978, I wrote what I called a *romanopera* [novelopera] that I called *L'Echarpe rouge* [The Red Scarf]. It was published by Maspero in 1979, and performed in Lyon, Avignon and then at the Palais de Chaillot in 1984 in the form of a real opera, with music by Georges Aperghis and directed by Antoine Vitez. This work followed, line by line, the schema of Claudel's *Soulier de Satin* (which Vitez directed in Avignon a few years later). Basically, I took up the challenge thrown down to popular theatre by

Claudel's creation of a form of theatre that was at once modern and Christian. And it is not for nothing that the title of Act II, Scene VI is *Choeur de la divisible défaite* [Chorus of the divisible defeat]. I will always remember the musical power of the chorus (all dressed in workers' overalls) while Pierre Vial – an exceptional actor – strode up and down the stage carrying an old umbrella and hesitantly murmuring, half-convinced, half-nostalgic: 'Communism! Communism!'

The scene has to be situated. The regional Party leadership in the working-class North East of the imaginary country in which the play is set has launched a sort of civil insurrection, and has, more specifically, called a general strike. That offensive gives the whole of the play's second act its title (The Autumn Offensive). It ends in complete failure and, after stormy discussions in all the revolutionary organizations, it is discussed, criticized and rejected in favour of military action on the part of the insurgents, this time under the leadership of the South of the country.

The scene I want to cite comes immediately after the failure of this premature 'autumn offensive'. It is set outside the gate of the SNOMA factory, early in the morning. The defeated workers are returning to work, heads bowed, between two lines of soldiers, managers and police. The workers' chorus was, according to the stage directions, born of this compact procession. The entire chorus has to do with how defeats can be divided and subsumed into a higher mode of thought. Here it is:

And so, one morning the colour of dead earth, we have once more lowered our banners very low and very solemnly. We have spurned our insurrection.

And so, here we are once more, the workers of SNOMA, in a town that has been bled try, heads bowed and defeated.

Once again, our efforts were not enough to force the outcome of the dispute.

The threshold of a reversal of positions.

I speak here of the interrogative prematurity of our watchful uprising.

I speak of the isolation of the proletariat in the undecided town, and of a far-away offensive.

I speak here of its failure, and the bitterness. But!

No one has the strength to make the mill of history run backwards for any length of time.

This is the time for both a reckoning and an understanding, the time of the tension through which, for the defeated,

The bad thing of failure turns into the combative excellence of knowledge [*un savoir*].

[. . .]

Join us, you, the defeated, the legendary defeated, with the fabulous sequel to your non-acceptances!

You! The oppressed of times gone by. Slaves of the sun-sacrifices who were mutilated for the splendour of tombs! The ploughmen who were sold, together with the earth that was the same colour as them! The children who have been expatriated into the bloody service of the cotton and the coal, now that the meadows have been fenced in.

Have you accepted this? No one ever accepts anything!

Spartacus, Jacquou le Croquant. Thomas Münzer!

And you: the tramps of the plains, the

Taiping rebels of the great loess, Chartists and Luddites, plotters from the labyrinth of the *banlieues*, egalitarian Babouvists, sans-culottes, Communards, Spartacists! All people from the popular sects and soviets of the sprawling *quartiers*, *sectionnaires* from the days of the Terror, men with forks and pikes, the men of the barricades and the burning chateaux! And the host of the many others who are violently striving to discover their plenitude,

And who, as they invent their plenitude, are at work in the continental shattering of history!

The sailors who threw their officers to carnivorous fish, the utopians of solar cities who opened fire in their territorial outposts, Quechua miners from the Andes with an appetite for dynamite! And the successive tidal waves of African rebels sheltering behind flaming leopard-skin shields in the colonial stench! Not forgetting the lone man who took down his hunting rifle and, like a suspicious wild boar, began to resist the aggressor in the forests of Europe.

And the deployment of great processions of

all kinds in the streets: sinister-looking students, girls demanding women's rights, the banners of great clandestine unions, old men rising up in memory of general strikes, nurses in their veils, and workers on bicycles!

Join us and give us the countless inventions and the multiform simplicity of people power: the mob orators and warriors of the peasant leagues, the *camisard* prophets, the women of the clubs, associations and federations, the workers and the *lycéens* of the *comités de base*, the action committees, the triple unions and the grand alliances! Factory soviets, soldiers' soviets, people's courts, the great village commissions formed to share out the land, to open an irrigation damn, or to form a militia! Revolutionary groups demanding price-controls, the execution of corrupt officials and for tight controls on food stocks!

And those, though they are few of them and this is a period that goes against the general trend, who cling to the correct idea in basements filled with the din of manual rotary presses. And then there are those who, armed with long bamboo poles, know how to skewer the fattest of police officers, and for whom everything else is a mystery.

All of you! Brothers of immense history! You look at our failure and you say: what are you giving up there? Didn't our failure extend beyond death itself? Didn't we fail interminably?

Let any man who dares to bring us before the court of that failure stand! And let him be beyond all shame!

We gave birth to your uncertain certitudes. And your strength in the imminence of victory is no more than the legacy of what we seemed to be doing.

And so, are you going to give up? Are you going to abolish our huge efforts, and the historical birth of our universal revenge,
In the reactionary verdict and bowed heads of the defeated?

No! I say, No!

The contented and the fearful are no concern of ours. It is the tenacious people's memory that creates the great hole in the world where the semaphore of communism has been planted century after century.

People of all times! People of all places! You are with us!

I would simply like to emphasize the relationship, which is spelled out in the summing up of the whole text, between the subjective possibility of getting over a defeat, and the vitality – both international and supra-temporal – of the communist hypothesis. A meditation on failure changes completely if we relate it not to the pure interiority – intellectual or tactical – of a politics, but to the link between that politics and its historicity. The thought of failure emerges at the point when a politics appears before the court of History, and when it sees itself there. And it is the communist hypothesis that represents and imagines the consistency of History.

3

At the beginning of the 1980s we were called to a different reckoning of what was going on. The 'red years' were well and truly over. The Mitterrand government conjured up all the old illusions and chimeras of the 'left', which consisted mainly in corrupting a fraction of the petty bourgeoisie by inviting it into the vicinity of power (even Deleuze accepted an invitation to dine with the President) and handing out credits to the 'associations' it was so keen on. 'Cultural policy' was a good name for this system of illusions. We had here a defeat without glory, and an unrecognizable failure in power. It was to last for over 20 years (probably until the present crisis) and its name was the Socialist Party. Oh! We ought to be able to say once more what Aragon, with the encouragement of Stalin, once said: 'Open fire on the dancing bears of Social Democracy!'[2] But no one even thinks of doing so.

On the other hand, it has to be said that the final convulsions of state socialism and the armed struggles associated with it were unbearably violent. The Red Guards of the Cultural Revolution were – as young people so often do when they are left to their own devices and obey the herd instinct – already committing countless crimes during the most confused

---

2   The allusion is to Louis Aragon's poem *Front Rouge* (1930). *Translator's note*.

moments of the Cultural Revolution. In Cambodia, the revolutionary Khmer Rouge thought they could use commandos of very young boys and girls drawn from the oppressed peasant masses, who had always been invisible, and who were suddenly given the power of life and death over anything that recalled the old society. Those young killers, whose descendants can still be seen today – especially in Africa – subjected the whole country to their reign of blind revenge, and devastated it without pity. In Peru, the methods used by Sendero Luminoso to forge the discipline of the rebellious Indian peasants were little different: 'Anyone I suspect of not being with me must be killed.' And the propaganda of the 'new philosophers' obviously made unlimited use of these terrifying episodes.

We were confronted with a sort of twofold notion of failure. We had before our very eyes the classic rightist failure: those who were weary of militant action rallied to the delights of parliamentary power, and the renegades made the transition from Maoism and active communism to the cosy home of the Socialist senator for the Gironde. But we could not forget the 'ultra-left' failure which, by handling every contradiction – even the slightest – with brutality and death, trapped the entire process within the dark limits of terror. This in fact seems to be unavoidable at times when the political dynamic of revolutions can no longer invent its becoming or assert itself for what it is. Even Robespierre had to fight on two fronts as 1794, and therefore his own failure, drew closer: against the *citra-révolutionaires*, or the rightists who followed Danton, and against the 'ultra-revolutionaries' and *enragés* who followed Hébert.

I devoted my play *L'Incident d'Antioche* to this problem. Once again, it follows the outline of a play by Claudel (*La Ville*), and it also uses the most important episodes in St Paul's mission, including the quarrel between Paul and Peter over the question of the universality of the gospel, which occurred in Antioch. The idea is that the revolutionary theme must not cling to a traditional particularity (to the rituals of being-Jewish in the case of the apostle Peter, or to the assumption that there is no alternative to the laws of the market economy and representative democracy in the case of today's renegades), and that the destruction of those particularities (Christian-inspired anti-Semitism or the Khmer Rouge's execution of the supporters of the old world) is not the only issue at stake. Universality, represented in the play by the character of Paula, presupposes that we resist our fascination with established powers, and our fascination with their pointless destruction. No peaceful continuation, and no ultimate sacrifice. Politics is a construct that certainly *separates* itself from whatever is dominant but it defends that separation – through violence if need be – only to the extent that, in the long term, it sheds light on the fact that it is only within the universal that we can all live under the rule of equality.

L'Incident d'Antioche describes a victorious and terribly destructive revolution whose leaders finally, and for the reasons I have just outlined, take the unheard-of decision to renounce the power they have won.

The first fragment I will cite here deals with Céphas's refusal to go on holding any post. He led the revolution, at the cost of terrible destruction. He is giving up because he loves only destruction, and because he prophesies that a new state is about to be reconstructed, built and created. And he is already bored with that prospect. He expresses himself thus:

Céphas. This is the end. I will lie down in the ashes of states. I will go away with the old texts.

Farewell, I am leaving, giving up.

Camille. What! Céphas! You can't leave things up in the air! You're not going to leave our undertaking leaderless in the midst of disaster and necessity!

David. Without any explanation! Without any critique! Turning your back when we should be picking up stones!

Céphas. I joined with you in the jurisdiction of command in order to do certain things, and we have done them. We hastened the decline of this country, which we took back to its terroristic origins.

The only thing that lies beyond victory is defeat. No, no! Not a sudden defeat and overthrow! The slow, irreversible defeat of that which has to come to terms with what exists.

Not the useless defeat that is covered in glory, not the legendary catastrophe. On the contrary: a useful and fertile defeat, the kind of defeat that brings back the peace of work and restores the might of the state.

I leave you the grandeur of that kind of defeat, not out of pride or lack of interest in its patience, but because I am ill-suited to it.

The orderliness of my idea of disorder now stands in the way of the imperative to build.

[. . .]

But let the lie be seen in all its clarity. In the clarity of what we have destroyed beneath our feet.

May the rubble embedded in the restoration maintain its hold over you, and may the stink

Persist!

Camille. Don't go, Céphas.

David. Stay. If power offends you, be the man who disturbs it.

Céphas. In the beginning, I enjoyed being a leader. These things are not to be scorned:

The circular, as short as a telegram from a lover, that brings *lycéens* who have dropped out of school to their feet on the other side of the country, or that foments a shop-floor uproar in the *banlieues*.

The ovations of the crowd as you stand on a platform in the summer, between the red flags and the portraits.

Or the ceasefire during the winter we spend in our tents.

But all that is over, and all that remains is the fear of the gaze.

That is why I will leave the circle, and chalk the word 'glory'.

As we can see, the failure for which Céphas finds himself so ill-suited is the rightist failure, the 'slow', inglorious failure of reconstructions and repetitions. The moment when we revert from revolution to state.

Paula is talking about the other failure – that of blind rage – when she enjoins her son, who has become leader after the departure of Céphas, to give up power. Here is the scene:

David. What exactly are you asking for?
Paula. I've told you. I'm asking you to give up power.
David. But why do you insist on using your maternal function for counter-revolutionary purposes?
Paula. You *are* the counter-revolution. You exhaust all trace of the will to justice. Your politics are vulgar.

David. And you are so distinguished.

Paula. Listen to me. Let me speak as though I were a man. Our hypothesis was not, in theory, that we were going to resolve the problem of good government. Isn't that so? We did not involve ourselves in the philosophers' speculations about the ideal state. We said that the world could stand the trajectory of a policy that could be reversed, a policy designed to put an end to politics. To domination, in other words. And you agreed with that.

David. I'm listening, professor.

Paula. It so happened that the historical realization of that hypothesis was swallowed up by the state. A liberating organization merged completely into the state. It has to be said that, when underground and at war, it devoted itself completely to the conquest of the state.

And so, the will to emancipation escaped its own origins. It must be *restored* to them.

David. What do you mean?

Paula. I mean it has to be *replaced*.

No correct policy can now argue that it is a continuation of the work that has already been done. Our mission is to unseal, once and for all, the consciousness that organizes justice, equality, the end of states and imperial rackets, and of the residual platform where the concern for power sucks in every form of energy.

What an impact it would have if you issued a proclamation of fidelity! In practice, that would mean returning to the path of the collective consciousness and its subjectivation! You would leave behind the state that loves its pomp, and its murderous stupidity.

David. We have left it behind, like an imperative that was more powerful than our will, the sacrifice of thousands of people, and our victory is its only meaning. Are we going to gather together all the dead in the summer of our absurdity, for one sublime abdication?

Paula. They've already played the *parti des fusillés* card.[3] What is the sense in placing the

---

3   *'Le parti des fusillés'* [the party of those who were shot] = the French Communist Party. The *fusillés* were those who were shot as resistance fighters during the Occupation. *Translator's note.*

meaning of politics under the jurisdiction of the dead? That bodes ill. And let me remind you that crowds of people are dying now, not for the sake of victory, but because of our victory. Whatever choice you make, you will be forced to select the corpses that justify your actions.

David. Where does this moral blackmail get us? Pity is pointless. When you are surrounded by devastation, reconstruction is the order of the day. If we have to borrow from the past, we will do so without any shame. Who can imagine that, after such a shock, the old state of affairs will emerge once more, as though nothing had happened? The world has changed for ever. You just have to trust it. My dear, dear mother, you see things from below. You are not one of the decision-makers.

Paula. That's an old trick, David. I am telling you that there is only one possible decision. Everything else is just a matter of using the brutal means at your disposal to manage constraints. Of course you'll do something new. You'll paint the surface of the sun grey.

David. Tell me precisely who you are. Are you

condemning what we have done? Are you on the side of the whites, of the scum that are lying low? I'm warning you: my heart is growing cold again.

Paula. You've done what had to be done. The little imperial beast has been exhausted, and is hiding out somewhere in the hills. You were the ones who sacrificed it. Thanks to you, the first cycle in the history of justice is now unbroken. That is why you must proclaim that a second power is emerging.

David. You're certainly not suggesting that we need more power. You're suggesting, on the contrary, that we renounce it, and for a long time to come.

Paula (*takes out a big sheet of paper and unfolds it*). Look at this military chart. My brother Claude Villembray gave it to me just before we had him put to death. There's the dream, there's the childhood. You really would have liked to conquer the world, just like any old king. Are you going to go on with that never-ending childish passion? Power is not the mark of the human race's greatness. The featherless biped must get a grip on himself and, unlikely as it seems, go against all the laws of nature and all the laws of history, and follow the path that means that anyone will be the equal of everyone. Not only in law, but in their material truth.

David. You're such a fanatic!

Paula. No, I'm not. On the contrary, I urge you to abandon all fanaticism. The decision you have to take has to be taken coldly. For anyone who gives in to the passion for images, it is incomprehensible. Forget about the obsession with conquest and the totality. Follow the thread of multiplicity.

(*Long silence*)

David. But, tell me Paula: how can we prevent everything from becoming dispersed and disunited if we make the unprecedented gesture you are suggesting?

Paula. Don't think I'm giving you a recipe. For such a long time, the impasse was that politics was centred on and represented by the state alone, so I am telling you to get out of that impasse, and to prove that the political truth circulates endlessly in a people that leans against the factory walls and finds shelter from the state in its inner strength.

It is like an event, as non-representable as the dramatic labour that makes the actions we see before us mysteriously unique.

David (*distraught*). But where do we begin something when you say that it has no beginning?

Paula. Find the people that matter. Listen to what they say. Organize their consistency, and aim for equality. Let there be nuclei of political conviction in the factory. Committees of the popular will in the estates and in the countryside. Let them transform that which exists, and let them be up to the generality of situations. Let their opposition to the state and the property-owning sharks be directly proportional to their immanent strength, and to the thought they wield.

David. That does not add up to a strategy.

Paula. The politics of the future can begin only if it gives its own formulation form and roots. Politics means uniting around a political vision that escapes the mental hold of the state. Don't ask me for anything more than this circle, which is the circle of any initial thought. We can found an era on a tautology. That is only natural. Parmenides laid the foundations for two thousand years of philosophy simply by proclaiming, with the requisite clarity, that being *is* and that non-being *is not*.

David. Politics means making politics *be*, so that the state will no longer *be*.

(*Silence*)

Paula. My son, my son! Do you want to trust yourself to this thought, in which, after an errant history, the old hypothesis, the old interpretation commits the same offence?

David. My head is spinning. I can see the undecidable clearly.

Paula. A politics, only one.

David. I trust myself to it.

Paula. I am confident that this politics is, thanks to me, real, escapes capture by the state, cannot be represented and is for ever being decoded.

I am confident that, when it follows the understanding of the will, what is so designated will gradually help the strength of a Subject to evade the rule of domination.

I know that this trajectory lies in the uniqueness of its consistency, and in the stubbornness of its subtlety.

I trust in the never-ending liberation, not as a chimera or as a smokescreen for despots, but as a figure and as an active combination, here and now, of that which gives man the capacity for something other than

The hierarchical economy of ants.

David (*expressionless*). All that. All that.

Paula. Strike hard, my son. That will give you confidence. Let the millennial struggle for power turn into the millennial struggle for its humiliation. For its final destruction.

David. Oh sovereign decision! The honour of an immoderate winter!

In the meantime, I urge you to be patient. But where is your place now, mother?

Paula. You can say that I did what I could do. Yes, you really can say that.

(*They embrace*)

We can see from all this that 'failing' is always very close to 'winning'. One of the great Maoist slogans of the 'red years' was 'Dare to struggle and dare to win.' But we know that it is not easy to follow that slogan when subjectivity is afraid, not of fighting, but of winning. Struggle exposes us to the simple form of failure (the assault did not succeed), while victory exposes us to its most redoubtable form: we notice that we have won in vain, and that our victory paves the way for repetition and restoration. That, for the state, a revolution is never anything more than an intervening period. Hence the sacrificial temptations of nothingness. For a politics of emancipation, the enemy that is to be feared most is not repression at the hands of the established order. It is the interiority of nihilism, and the unbounded cruelty that can come with its emptiness.

4

If we look at things in less poetic, more descriptive and more historical terms, we will probably find that the becoming of the politics of emancipation meets with not two, but three different forms of failure.

The best known, or the most circumscribed, is the

failure of an attempt in which revolutionaries who have briefly taken power over a country or a zone and tried to establish new laws are crushed by an armed counter-revolution. Very many insurrections come into this category, and the best-known examples in the twentieth century are probably the Spartacist insurrection after the First World War, in which Rosa Luxemburg and Karl Liebknecht perished, and those in Shanghai and Canton in China in the 1920s. The problem raised by this type of failure is always that of the 'balance of power'. It comes down to a problem that combines, on the one hand, the degree to which the people's detachments are organized and, on the other, the opportuneness of the moment where the dis-organization of the might of the state is concerned. In the short term, a positive assessment of the defeat will discuss the new disciplines that are required if the insurrection is to succeed. At a later stage, the debate will be more contentious and will centre on the insurgents' ability to rally the broad masses of the 'civilian' population. The paradigmatic example of such discussions is the history of the various assessments that have been made of the Paris Commune. That debate has been going on ever since

Marx. It has involved Marx, Lissagaray, Lenin and the Chinese revolutionaries in about 1981, and it still continues today. The third study in the present collection re-opens the file.

The second type of failure is that of a broad movement involving disparate but very large forces whose goal is not really the seizure of power, even though they have forced the reactionary forces of the state on to the defensive for long periods of time. When such a movement retreats because the old order, or at least its general outline, has been restored, we have to understand the nature of its actions, and their implications. Between the idea that it was all imaginary and the idea that it represented a decisive break in our conception of what is to be done and of what a politics of liberation is, there is a whole range of possibilities. The Fronde of the early sixteenth century in France was, perhaps, the first example of this type of movement. The 1911 movement in China also displays many of the same features. A more recent model is, of course, the mythical May '68, which gave rise to countless publications and furious discussions on its fortieth anniversary. The first study in this volume is devoted to it.

The third type of failure concerns an attempt to transform a state that officially declares itself to be socialist, and to bring it into line with the idea of a free association, which, ever since Marx, has always seemed to be stipulated by the communist hypothesis. In such cases, the failure is that the outcome takes us in the opposite direction: either the terrorism of the party-state is restored, any reference to socialism, and a fortiori communism, is abandoned, or the state rallies to the non-egalitarian constraints of capitalism, or both those things happen, as one paves the way for the other. There have been what might be called 'weak' forms of this kind of attempt, as when Czechoslovakia's 'socialism with a human face' was crushed by the Soviet army in 1968. And there have been much more significant forms, such as Poland's Solidarity workers' movement between 14 August 1980 (when the strike began in Gdansk's shipyards) and 13 December 1981 (when the state of emergency was declared). The truly revolutionary form, which inspired the whole of French Maoism between 1965 and 1976, was the GPCR (Great Proletarian Cultural Revolution) in China, at least during its truly mass and open phase between 1966 and 1968. Chapter II in the present book is devoted to it.

5

The word 'communism', together with the general
hypothesis that it can imply effective political
procedures, is now back in circulation. A conference
under the general title of 'The Idea of Communism'
was held in London on 13–15 March 2009. This
conference calls for two essential comments.
First of all, in addition to the two people behind
it (Slavoj Žižek and myself), the great names of
the true philosophy of our times (by which I mean
a philosophy that is not reducible to academic
exercises or support for the ruling order) were
strongly represented. Over a period of three days,
the conference heard contributions from Judith
Balso, Bruno Bosteels, Terry Eagleton, Peter
Hallward, Michael Hardt, Toni Negri, Jacques
Rancière, Alessandro Russo, Alberto Toscano and
Gianni Vattimo. Jean-Luc Nancy and Wang Hui had
agreed to speak but were prevented from doing so by
external circumstances. All had carefully read the

proviso to which all participants had to subscribe:
whatever their approach, they had to agree that the
word 'communism' can and must now acquire a
positive value once more. My second remark is that
the Birkbeck Institute for the Humanities, which
hosted this event on a temporary basis, had to hire a
huge lecture theatre holding one thousand people in
order to accommodate the audience, which consisted
mainly of young people. This shared enthusiasm on
the part of both the philosophers and their audience
for a word that was sentenced to death by public
opinion almost 30 years ago surprised everyone. My
own contribution is appended to this dossier on the
communist hypothesis.

6

This book is, I insist, a book of philosophy.
Appearances notwithstanding, it does not deal directly
with either politics (though it does refer to politics) or
political philosophy (even though it suggests a sort of
link between the political condition and philosophy).

A political text is something internal to an organized political process. It expresses its thought, deploys its forces and announces its initiatives. A text on political philosophy – a discipline I have always asserted to be futile – claims to 'found' politics, or even 'the political', and to impose upon it norms that are, ultimately, moral norms: 'good' power, the 'good' state, 'good' democracy and so on. And besides, political philosophy is now nothing more than the erudite servant of capitalo-parliamentarianism. What interests me here is very different. My examination of the particularities of the notion of failure in politics represents an attempt to define the generic form taken by all truth processes when they come up against obstacles that are inherent in the world in which they operate. The underlying formalization of this problem is the concept of 'point' described in Book VI of my *Logics of Worlds*. A point is a moment within a truth procedure (such as a sequence of emancipatory politics) when a binary choice (do this *or* that) decides the future of the entire process. Many examples of points will be found in the studies that follow. We have to realize that almost all failures have to do with the fact that a point has been badly

handled. Any failure can be located *in a point*. And
that is why any failure is a lesson which, ultimately,
can be incorporated into the positive universality of
the construction of a truth. Before that can be done,
the point over which the choice proved to be disastrous
must be located, found and reconstructed. Using the
old terminology, we can say that the universal lesson
of a failure lies in the correlation between a tactical
decision and a strategic impasse. But if we abandon
the military lexicon, we can say that the question of
the point masks the fundamental statement: when a
truth is at stake, failure cannot be theorized on the
basis of a tautology. We have a magnificent theorem
about worlds, whatever they are: the points of a world
form a topological space. Which means, in ordinary
language, that the difficulties of a politics are never
universal, as enemy propaganda – along the lines of
'your communist hypothesis is nothing more than a
chimera that cannot be put into practice, a utopia
that has nothing to do with the real world' – would
always have us believe in order to discourage us once
and for all. Its difficulties are caught up in a network
in which it is possible, although often difficult, to
know their place, what surrounds them, and how to

approach them. We can therefore speak of a *space of possible failures*. And it is within that space that a failure invites us to seek and to theorize the point at which we are now forbidden to fail.

I

We Are Still the Contemporaries of May '68

*T*here are three parts to this set of essays on May '68. The first is a lecture given in Clermont-Ferrand in 2008 at the invitation of the 'Les Amis du temps des cerises' association in 2008. The second is an article written 'in the heat of the moment' in July 1968 and published by the Belgian journal Textures *(nos. 3–4) in the winter of 1968. The third is the full version of an article on capitalism's systemic crisis published in a shortened version by the daily* Le Monde *in late 2008. I reproduce it here because the two earlier texts deal mainly with the question of capitalism and its parliamentary political organization.*

1

May '68 Revisited, 40 Years On

I would like to begin by asking a very simple question: why all this fuss about May '68 – articles, broadcasts, discussions and commemorations of all kinds–40 years after the event? There was nothing of the kind for the thirtieth or twentieth anniversary.

The first answer is decidedly pessimistic. We can now commemorate May '68 because we are convinced that it is dead. Forty years after the event, there is no life left in it. Or so say some who were once the *notables* of '68. 'Forget Mai 68', Cohn-Bendit tells us, now that he has become an ordinary politician. We are living in a very different world, the situation has changed completely, and we can therefore commemorate the best years of our lives with a clear conscience. Nothing that happened then has any active significance for us. Nostalgia and folklore.

There is also a second and even more pessimistic

answer. We are commemorating May '68 because the real outcome and the real hero of '68 is unfettered neo-liberal capitalism. The libertarian ideas of '68, the transformation of the way we live, the individualism and the taste for *jouissance* have become a reality thanks to post-modern capitalism and its garish world of all sorts of consumerism. Ultimately, Sarkozy himself is the product of May '68, and to celebrate May '68, as André Glucksmann invites us to do, is to celebrate the neo-liberal West that the American army is so bravely defending against the barbarians.

I would like to contrast these depressing visions with some more optimistic hypotheses about what we are commemorating.

The first is that this interest in '68, especially on the part of significant numbers of young people, is, on the contrary, an anti-Sarkozy reflex. Even as its importance is being denied so strongly, we appear to be looking back at May '68 because it is a potential source of inspiration, a sort of historical poem that gives us new courage and that allows us really to react now that we are in the depths of despair.

And then there is another, and even more optimistic, hypothesis. This commemoration, and even the official, commodified and deformed side of it, may mask the vague idea that a different political and societal world is possible, that the great idea of radical change, which for 200 years went by the name of 'revolution' and which has haunted the people of this country for 40 years now, is still quietly spreading, despite the official pretence that it has been completely defeated.

But we have to go further back.

We have to understand one essential point: the reason why this commemoration is complicated and gives rise to contradictory hypotheses is that May '68 itself was an event of great complexity. It is impossible to reduce it to a conveniently unitary image. I would like to transmit to you this internal division, the heterogeneous multiplicity that was May '68.

There were in fact four different 'May '68s'. The strength and the distinctive feature of the French May '68 is that it entwined, combined and superimposed four processes that are, in the final analysis, quite heterogeneous. And the reason why interpretations of that event differ so much is that they usually recall one aspect of it and not the complex totality that gives it its true grandeur.

Let us unpack this complexity.

May '68 was primarily an uprising, a revolt, on the part of young university and school students. That is its most spectacular and best-known aspect, the one that has left the most powerful images, and which we have recently been revisiting: the mass demonstrations, the barricades, the battles with the police, and so on. It seems to me that we have to extract three characteristics from these images of the violence of the repression and the enthusiasm. First, this uprising was at the time a worldwide phenomenon (Mexico, Germany, China, Italy, the USA . . .). It was therefore not a specifically French phenomenon. Second, it has to be remembered that the university and school students represented a minority of young people. In the 1960s, between 10 and 15 per cent of the age cohort took the *baccalauréat*. When we talk about 'university and school students', we are talking about a small fraction of young people, and they were very cut off from the broad masses of working-class youth. Third, the novel elements came into two categories. On the one hand: the extraordinary strength of the ideology and the symbols, the Marxist vocabulary and the idea of revolution. On the other: the acceptance of violence. It may well have been defensive and anti-repressive, but it was still violence. That is what gave the revolt its particular flavour. All this makes up one May '68.

The second, and very different, May '68 was the biggest general strike in the whole of French history. In many respects, it was a classic general strike. It was structured around the big factories, and organized mainly by the unions, and especially the CGT. Its point of reference was the last great strike of this type, namely the Popular Front. We might say that, given its scale and its general features, the strike took place, in historical terms, in a very different context from the youth rebellion. It belongs to a context that I would describe as being more classically 'on the left'. Having said that, it too was inspired by radically innovative elements. There are three such elements.

First, the strike call and the decision to strike had, in general, little to do with official working-class institutions. In most cases, the movement was launched by groups of young workers outside the big union organizations, which then rallied to it, partly in a bid to take control of it. There was then in the workers' May '68 an element of revolt that was also internal to youth. These young workers used what were often described as 'wildcat strikes' to distinguish them from the unions' traditional 'days of action'. It should be noted that these wild cat strikes began as early as 1967, and that the workers' May '68 was not simply an effect of the students' May '68, for it anticipated the latter. This temporal and historical link between a movement organized by educated young people and a workers' movement is quite unusual. Second radical element: the systematic use of factory occupations. This was obviously an inheritance of the great strikes of 1936 and 1947, but it took place on a wider scale. Almost all the factories were occupied and decked with red flags. Now that is a great image! You have to have seen what this country looked like with all the factories flying red flags. No one who saw it will ever forget it. Third 'hard' element: at this time and in the years that followed, the systematic practice of kidnapping bosses, and peripheral battles with 'security' or the CRS. This means that the point I was speaking about just now

– a certain acceptance of violence – existed not only within the school and university youth movement, but also within the workers' movement. And finally, it has to be remembered, to end our discussion of the second May '68, that, given all these elements, the question of how long the movement should last and how it should be controlled was acute. There was a contradiction between the CGT's desire to take control, and practices that were steeped in what the historian Xavier Vigna calls 'working-class insubordination', and there were conflicts within the strike movement.[4] They could be very sharp, and they are still symbolized by the Renault-Billancourt workers' rejection of the protocols negotiated at Grenelle. Something rebelled against the attempts to find a classic negotiated settlement to the general strike.

There is a third, and equally heterogeneous, May '68. I will describe it as the libertarian May. It concerns the question of the changing moral climate, of changing sexual relations and of

4   See Xavier Vigna, *L'insubordination ouvrière dans les années 68. Essai d'histoire politique des usines*, Presses Universitaires de Rennes, 2007. *Translator's note.*

individual freedom. That question was to give rise to
the women's movement, and then the movement for
homosexual rights and emancipation. It would also
have an impact on the cultural sphere, with the idea
of a new theatre, new forms of political expression,
a new style of collective action, the promotion
of happenings and improvisation, and the *états
généraux du cinéma*. This too constitutes a distinctive
component of May '68, which we can describe as
ideological, and while it did sometimes degenerate
into a snobbish and party-going anarchism, it was
still in keeping with the general mood of the event.
One has only to think of the graphic power of posters
that were designed in the studios of the Ecole des
beaux-arts in May.

It has to be recalled that these three components
remained distinct, even though there were major
overlaps between them. There could be significant
conflicts between them. There were real clashes
between *gauchisme* and the classic left, as well
as between political *gauchisme* (represented by
Trotskyism and Maoism) and cultural *gauchisme*,
which tended to be anarchistic. All this produces an
image of May '68 as a contradictory effervescence, and

by no means a unitary festival. In May '68, political life was intense, and it was lived in the midst of a multiplicity of contradictions.

These three components were represented by great symbolic sites: the occupied Sorbonne for students, the big car plants (and especially Billancourt) for workers, and the occupation of the Odéon theatre for the libertarian May.

Three components, three sites, three types of symbolism and discourse and therefore, 40 years after the event, three different reckonings. What are we talking about when we talk about May '68 today? About the whole event, or about one isolated component?

I would like to argue that none of these components is the most important, because there was a fourth May '68. This May was crucial, and it still prescribes what the future will bring. It is more difficult to read because it unfolded over time and was not an instantaneous explosion. It is what came after the merry month of May, and it produced some intense political years. Although difficult to grasp if we stick closely to the initial circumstances, it dominated the period between 1968 and 1978, and was then repressed and absorbed by the victory of the Union of the Left and the miserable 'Mitterrand years'. We would do better to speak of a ''68 decade' rather than of 'May '68'.

There are two aspects to the process of the fourth May '68. First, there is the conviction that, from the 1960s onwards, we were witnessing the end of an old conception of politics. Followed by a somewhat halting search for a new conception of politics throughout the decade 1970–80. The difference between this fourth element and the first three is that it was completely obsessed with the question: 'What is politics?' It was at once a very theoretical and very difficult question, but it was also a product of the many immediate experiments to which people committed themselves with such enthusiasm.

The old conception we were trying to break away from at this time was based on the dominant idea (shared by activists of all kinds and in that sense universally accepted inside the 'revolutionary' camp) that there is such a thing as a historical agent offering a possibility of emancipation. It was variously known as the working class, the proletariat and sometimes the people, and though there were debates as to its composition and its size, everyone agreed that it existed. The shared conviction that there is an 'objective' agent inscribed in social reality, and that it offers the possibility of emancipation, is probably the biggest difference between then and now. In the meantime, we have had the bleak 1980s. At the time, we assumed that the politics of emancipation was neither a pure idea, an expression of the will nor a moral dictate, but that it was inscribed in, and almost programmed by, historical and social reality. One of that conviction's implications was that this objective agent had to be transformed into a subjective power, that a social entity had to become a subjective actor. For that to happen, it had to be represented by a specific organization, and that is precisely what we called a party, a working-class or people's party. That party had to be present wherever there were sites of power or intervention. There were certainly wide-ranging discussions about what that party was. Did it already exist, or did it have to be created or re-created? What form would it take? And so on. But there was a basic agreement that there was a historical agent, and that that agent had to be organized. That political organization obviously had a social basis in mass organizations that plunged their roots into an immediate social reality. Which raised the whole question of the role of trade unionism, of its relationship with the party, and of what was meant by a unionism based on the class struggle.

This gave us something that still survives today: the idea that there are two sides to emancipatory political action. First, there are social movements bound up with particular demands. The unions are their natural organizations. Then there is the party element, which consists in being present in all possible sites of power, and of bringing to them, if I can put it this way, the strength and content of the social movements.

This is what might be called the classic conception. In '68, that conception was broadly shared by all actors, and everyone spoke the same language. No matter whether they were actors in dominant institutions or protesters [*contestataires*], orthodox communists or *gauchistes*, Maoists or Trotskyists, everyone used the vocabulary of classes, class struggles, the proletarian leadership of struggles, mass organizations and the party. There were, of course, violent disagreements about the legitimacy and significance of these movements. But everyone spoke the same language, and the red flag was everyone's emblem. I insist that, despite its vehement contradictions, May '68 was united under the red flag. May '68 was the last time – at least until today and probably, alas, tomorrow – the red flag flew over the country, the factories and the neighbourhoods. Nowadays, we scarcely dare to unfurl it. Towards the end of the month of May, in 1968, it could even be seen flying from the windows of the apartments of a fraction of the bourgeoisie.

But the secret truth, which was gradually revealed, is that this common language, symbolized by the red flag, was in fact dying out. There was a basic ambiguity about May '68: a language that was spoken by all was beginning to die out. There is a sort of temporary lack of distinction between what is beginning and what is coming to an end, and it is this that gives May '68 its mysterious intensity.

It was, in practical terms, beginning to die because May '68, and even more so the years that followed, was a huge challenge to the legitimacy of the historical organizations of the Left, of unions, parties and famous leaders. Even in the factories, discipline, the usual form of strikes, the labour hierarchy and the unions' authority over the movements were being challenged. Working-class or popular action might at any moment break out of its normal framework and appear in the form of what were seen as anarchic or wildcat initiatives. And, perhaps more important still, there was a radical critique of representative democracy, of the parliamentary and electoral framework, and of 'democracy' in the state, institutional and constitutional form. We must not forget, finally, that May '68's last slogan was *élections piège à cons* ['Elections are a con']. And it was not just an ideological craze. There were specific reasons for this hostility to representative democracy. After a month of student and then unprecedented working-class and popular mobilizations, the government succeeded in organizing elections, and the result was the most reactionary Chamber of Deputies anyone had ever seen. It then became clear to everyone that the electoral *dispositif* is not just, or even primarily, a representative *dispositif*: it is also a *dispositif* that represses movements, anything that is new, and anything that tries to break away from it.

All this – all that 'great critique', to use the language of the Chinese revolutionaries, and it was essentially negative – helped to convey a new vision, a vision of politics that was trying to wrench itself away from the old vision. The attempt to do that is what I call the fourth May '68. The fourth May '68 is seeking to find that which might exist beyond the confines of classic revolutionism. It seeks it blindly because it uses the same language as the language that dominated the conception it was trying to get away from. Hence the (obviously inadequate) thematic of 'betrayal' or 'renunciation': traditional organizations were supposedly betraying their own language. They were – to use the beautiful, colourful language of the Chinese once more – 'raising the red flag to fight the red flag'. The reason why we Maoists called the Parti Communiste Français and its satellites 'revisionist' is that we thought, in the same way that Lenin thought of the Social-Democrats Bernstein and Kautsky, that these organizations were turning the Marxist language they seemed to be using into its opposite. What we failed to see at the time was that it was the language itself that had to be transformed, but this time in an affirmative sense. All these images of a possible link between these different Mays were our centre of gravity as we searched so blindly. The fourth May is the diagonal that links the other three. All the new initiatives

that allowed us to circulate between these three
heterogeneous movements, and especially between
the student movement and the workers' movement,
were our treasure-trove.

At this point, we need to use more colourful
language.

At the time May '68 was getting under way, I was
a lecturer in Reims. The university (which was in
fact a small university centre where a first-year
foundation course was about the only thing on offer)
went on strike. So one day we organized a march to
the Chausson factory, which was the biggest factory
in town to have gone on strike. That sunny day, we
marched in a long, compact procession towards
the factory. What were we going to do when we got
there? We didn't know, but had a vague idea that the
student revolt and the workers' strike should unite,
without the intermediary of the classic organizations.
We approached the barricaded factory, which was
decked with red flags, with a line of trade unionists
standing outside the gates, which had been welded
shut. They looked at us with mingled hostility and
suspicion. A few young workers came up to us, and
then more and more of them. Informal discussions

got under way. A sort of local fusion was taking place. We agreed to get together to organize joint meetings in town. The meetings went ahead, and became the matrix for the establishment of the 'Chausson solidarity fund'. This was something completely new and had links with the Union des Communistes de France marxiste-léniniste (UCFml), the Maoist organization established in late 1969 by Natacha Michel, Sylvain Lazarus, myself and a fair number of young people.

What happened at the gates of the Chausson factory would have been completely improbable, even unimaginable, a week earlier. The solid union and party *dispositif* usually kept workers, young people and intellectuals strictly apart in their respective organizations. The local or national leadership was the only mediator. We found ourselves in a situation in which that *dispositif* was falling apart before our very eyes. This was something completely new, and we were both immediate actors and bewildered spectators. This was an event in the philosophical sense of the term: something was happening but its consequences were incalculable. What were its consequences during the ten 'red years' between

1968 and 1978? Thousands of students, high school students, workers, women from the estates and proletarians from Africa went in search of a new politics. What would a political practice that was not willing to keep everyone in their place look like? A political practice that accepted new trajectories, impossible encounters, and meetings between people who did not usually talk to each other? At that point, we realized, without really understanding it, that if a new emancipatory politics was possible, it would turn social classifications upside down. It would not consist in organizing everyone in the places where they were, but in organizing lightning displacements, both material and mental.

I have just told you the story of a blind displacement. What inspired us was the conviction that we had to do away with places. That is what is meant, in the most general sense, by the word 'communism': an egalitarian society which, acting under its own impetus, brings down walls and barriers; a polyvalent society, with variable trajectories, both at work and in our lives. But 'communism' also means forms of political organization that are not modelled on spatial hierarchies. That is what the fourth May '68 was: all those experiments were testimony to the fact that an impossible upheaval was taking place. It was politically possible to change places, thanks to a new kind of *prise de la parole* and the tentative search for forms of organization adequate to the novelty of the event.

Ten years later, the process of the Union of the Left and the election of Mitterrand partly repressed all that, and seemed to impose a return to the classical model. We went back to the 'everyone in their place' typical of that model: the parties of the left govern when they can, the unions put forward demands, the intellectuals intellectualize, the workers are in the factories, and so on. As in all returns to order, the misadventures of a 'left' that was in reality already dead fostered a short-lived illusion amongst broad fractions of the people at the very beginning of the 1980s, between 1980 and 1983. The left could not give politics a new lease of life; it was a ghost, and it smelled strongly of decay. We saw that very clearly with the 'austerity' regime of 1982–83, when the workers who went on strike at Talbot were described as Shi'ite terrorists, when the detention centres were opened, when laws were passed to put an end to family immigration, and when the Prime Minister Pierr Bérégovoy embarked upon an unprecedented financial liberalization that began by making France part of a ferocious globalized capitalism (for the systemic crisis in its ferocity, see below).

Having closed that parenthesis, we can say that we are still struggling with the difficult questions raised by May '68. We are the contemporaries of '68 from the point of view of politics, the definition of politics, and the organized future of politics. I therefore use the word 'contemporary' in the strongest possible sense. Of course, the world has changed, and of course categories have changed. The categories 'student youth', 'workers' and 'peasants' now mean something different, and the union and party organizations of those days are now in ruins. But *we have the same problem*, and are the contemporaries of the problem revealed by May '68: the classical figure of the politics of emancipation was ineffective. Those of us who were politically active in the 1960s and 1970s did not need the collapse of the USSR to teach us that. Countless new things have been experimented with, tried out and tested both in theory and in the practices that are dialectically bound up with it. And it still goes on thanks to the energy of a handful of activists, intellectuals and workers – and no distinction is made between them – who appear to be working in isolation. They are the guardians of the future and they are inventing the future. But it cannot be said that the problem has been resolved: what new forms of political organization are needed to handle political antagonisms? As in science, until such time as the problem has not been resolved, you have all sorts of discoveries stimulated by the search for a solution. Sometimes, and for the same reason, whole new theories see the light of day, but the problem itself is still there. We can define our contemporaneity with May '68 in similar terms. It is another way of talking about our fidelity to May '68.

The decisive issue is the need to cling to the historical hypothesis of a world that has been freed from the law of profit and private interest – even while we are, at the level of intellectual representations, still prisoners of the conviction that we cannot do away with it, that this is the way of the world, and that no politics of emancipation is possible. That is what I propose to call the communist hypothesis. It is in fact mainly negative, as it is safer and more important to say that the existing world is not *necessary* than it is to say, when we have nothing to go on, that a different world is possible. This is a question of modal logic: how, in political terms, can we move from non-necessity to possibility? Because quite simply, if we accept the inevitability of the unbridled capitalist economy and the parliamentary politics that supports it, then we quite simply cannot *see* the other possibilities that are inherent in the situation in which we find ourselves.

Second, we have to try to retain the words of our language, even though we no longer dare to say them out loud. In '68, these were the words that were used by everyone. Now they tell us: 'The world has changed, so you can no longer use those words, and you know that it was the language of illusions and terror.' 'Oh yes, we can! And we must!' The problem is still there, and that means that we must be able to pronounce those words. It is up to us to criticise them, and to give them a new meaning. We must be able to go on saying 'people', 'workers', 'abolition of private property', and so on, without being considered has-beens, and without considering ourselves as has-beens. We have to discuss these words in our own field, in our own camp. We have to put an end to the linguistic terrorism that delivers us into the hands of our enemies. Giving up on the language issue, and accepting the terror that subjectively forbids us to pronounce words that offend dominant sensibilities, is an intolerable form of oppression.

And finally, we have to realize that all politics is organized, and that the most difficult question is probably that of what type of organization we need. We can resolve it through the multifaceted experiments that begin in '68. For the classic party *dispositif*, and its social supports, the most important 'battles' were in fact electoral battles, and that is a doctrine that has given all it can give. It is worn out and no longer works, despite the great things it was able to achieve or promote between 1900 and 1960.

We have to discuss our fidelity to May '68 on two levels. At the ideological and historical level, we should draw up our own balance sheet for the twentieth century, so that we can reformulate the emancipation hypothesis in contemporary terms, now that the socialist states have failed. And we also know that new local experiments and political battles are going on, and that they will provide the backdrop that will create these new forms of organization.

This combination of complex ideological and historical work, and theoretical and practical data about new forms of political organization, is the defining feature of our times. I would readily describe this as *the era of the reformulation of the communist hypothesis*. Then what is the virtue that means most to us? You know that the revolutionaries of 1792–94 used the word 'virtue'. Saint-Just asked the crucial question: 'What do those who want neither virtue nor terror want?' His answer was that they wanted corruption. And that indeed is what today's world asks of us: to accept the wholesale corruption of minds under the yoke of commodities and money. The main political virtue we need to fight that now is courage. Not only courage when we face the police – though we will certainly find that – but the courage to defend and practice our ideas and principles, to say what we think, what we want, and what we are doing.

To put it in a nutshell: we have to be bold enough to have an idea. A great idea. We have to convince ourselves that there is nothing ridiculous or criminal about having a great idea. The world of global and arrogant capitalism in which we live is taking us back to the 1840s and the birth of capitalism. Its imperative, as formulated by Guizot, was: 'Get rich!' We can translate that as 'Live without an idea!' We have to say that we cannot live without an idea. We have to say: 'Have the courage to support the idea, and it can only be the communist idea in its generic sense.' That is why we must remain the contemporaries of May '68. In its own way, it tells us that living without an idea is intolerable. And then a long and terrible resignation set in. Too many people now think that there is no alternative to living for oneself, for one's own interests. Let us have the courage to cut ourselves off from such people. I am a philosopher, so let me tell you something that has been said again and again since Plato's day. It is very simple. I am telling you as a philosopher that we have to live with an idea, and that what deserves to be called a real politics begins with that conviction.

2

Outline of a Beginning

I am deeply grateful to my friend David Faroult, first for having rediscovered this text, which was published in late 1968 in the Belgian journal Textures *— and of which I had only vague memories — and, second, for agreeing to let me publish it here, even though I had granted him exclusive rights for its future publication in a journal.*

On rereading a text that really was written 'in the heat of the moment' or just after what the Chinese Red Guards called the 'revolutionary storm', I am struck by three things. The first is that, even though the analysis uses somewhat dated categories (fairly conventional class divisions, a somewhat vague use of the word 'ideology', a dated evocation of Marxist–Leninist 'science' . . .), it is still readable and relevant. It in fact demonstrates the consistency of the movement and the forms of its failure, the main reasons for being on its side and, as we look to the future, the main reasons that explain its considerable weaknesses. The other very striking thing about it is the extent of the subjective regression that was organized between the end of the period ushered in by May '68 (somewhere in the mid-1970s) and today. The text asks, with some irony, who would be so bold as to go on saying (in the summer of 1968) that the West is freedom's bulwark? Today, many people, many intellectuals, would, alas, unhesitatingly endorse that stupid statement. The third striking thing about it is that it takes no account of the one thing that proves to be the key to everything: the obsolescence of a strict Leninism centred upon the question of the party, which, precisely because it is centred on the party, continues to subordinate politics to its statist deviation. It is clear that the question of organization, which is the only thing that can bring about political and practical unity between disparate groups, is indeed central to the lessons of May '68. The 'movement' itself resolves none of the problems it helps to raise in a historical sense. But in the text I wrote at the time, the syntagm 'Marxist–Leninist party' serves as the key to everything. Shortly after it was written, some friends and I wrote, as it happens, a pamphlet entitled

'Towards a Marxist–Leninist Party of a New Kind'.[5]
*The formula 'of a new kind' is an obvious indication
that we had some doubts. It is in fact the party form
itself that has to be abandoned: the Stalinist period
demonstrated that it could not deal with the very
problems that arose from its victorious use in Russia
in 1917 and in China in 1949. And the Cultural
Revolution, which is mentioned in passing in a text
that focuses on the problems of the student movement,
demonstrates its ultimate limitations. Although the
workers and intellectual youth rebelled against the
party, their rebellion failed to change the party itself,
even though, when asked where the bourgeoisie was
in a socialist country, Mao had replied: 'right inside
the Communist Party itself'. The bourgeoisie had
indeed found a convenient hiding place inside the
party, and the means to forge its new power, as we can
see from China today, now that it has embarked upon
a nineteenth-century form of capital accumulation.*

---

5 *Contribution au problème de la construction d'un parti
marxiste-léniniste de type nouveau*, A. Badiou, H. Jancovici,
D. Menetrey, E. Terray; published in 1969 by F. Maspero.
Translator's note.

The great movement of May '68 has to be reread in the light of the obvious conclusion: that the 'class party' is at once a glorious formula and one that has become exhausted. The question of the new forms that an emancipatory political discipline will take is the central question of the communism to come.

The people, and the people alone, are the active force in the making of world history, while we ourselves are often childish and ignorant.

Mao Zedong

Even before the movement got under way, there was the age-old contradiction that is inherent in the capitalist university. Long before us, France (1848), Russia (1905–17), China (1919), Latin America and Japan saw heroic student mass uprisings against the bourgeois dictatorship. Elsewhere as in Mexico, the Fathers succeeded in safeguarding their own interests from the brutal demands of the Sons, which just goes to prove that the obstacle is fragile: provocations, guns and blood.

On the one hand, the growing incorporation of science into the productive forces demands a general heightening of the theoretical consciousness of the masses; at the same time, the enjoyment of the goods that are distributed (leisure, 'cultural' goods, complex objects) presupposes some sort of understanding of the constraints, of the effects of listening to and reading adverts, an awareness of sophisticated stimuli, etc.; the bourgeoisie to some extent relies for its politico-social defence upon the ideology of a *gap* between the middle strata (employees, cadres, supervisors, civil servants) and the proletariat. If these two groups united in any practical sense, it would pose a deadly threat to the employers' class power. Now, the awareness of that gap is conveyed by 'culture' and supported by the cornerstone of the academic edifice: the distinction between intellectual labour and manual labour. It is therefore essential to educate the 'middle strata' on a mass but *differentiated* basis: giving them a taste of secondary, or even higher, education marks in indelible terms their sense of distance and their fear of being proletarianized.

On the other hand, the domination of bourgeois *ideology* must be preserved by all means – or, failing that, the domination of its stand-in amongst the popular masses: petty-bourgeois and social-democratic ideology. Now that domination is to a large extent based upon organized ignorance. Long instilled by religious institutions, that ignorance safeguarded, thanks to the obscurantism it fostered amongst the peasant masses, the cornerstone of the French bourgeoisie's strategy from 1794 onwards: an alliance with rural producers. In the towns, this task was to some extent delegated to secular educational apparatuses. The educational system was therefore the institution that was always given the task of overcoming the following contradiction: *how can the theoretical consciousness of ever-expanding groups be heightened without calling into question the supremacy of bourgeois ideology, which is based upon ignorance and intellectual repression?*

There were two solutions to this problem:

1. The elite were, in so far as it was possible, selected by a form of education that gave a free rein to family determinisms, or, in other words, the determinism of class origins; at the same time, things were so ordered that the selection criteria (the rules of 'talking proper', the ability to handle clichés, the pseudo-scientific structure of the 'problem', speed of execution and a rapid assessment of problems) were closely bound up

with ceremonies specific to bourgeois ideology, and especially private politeness.

2. 'Pure' theoretical practice (the sciences) was divorced from ideological education (the humanities) as though they were two different essences, and everyone was required to choose between the two on the basis of their so-called 'gifts', which the system took upon itself to detect. The long-term implication of this 'choice' was that science itself was made subservient to the vague humanism in which 'liberal' thought languished. As a rule, no one is more blind to the critical powers of science than a scientist. No one is better prepared by the educational apparatuses for slavery than an 'expert' or agent of a defined specialism.

In France, this system finds its apotheosis in the aristocratism of the scientific *grandes écoles*, the mangers where the high bourgeoisie feeds, and where science, in the bastardized and stereotypical form of the 'cramming' characteristic of *les classes préparatoires*, goes hand in hand with the meticulous organization of ideological stupidity.

And yet these protective arrangements appear to have come under threat from all sides in recent years.

The main reason for that is, of course, that the system could not prevent the emergence of mass *lycées* and universities: the development of the productive forces required them. As a result, a broad fraction of the progressive petty bourgeoisie (that fraction which, because it is excluded from power, is tempted to forge links with the proletariat) gained access to higher education, and brought more and more pressure to bear on its servile academicism. The decadent character of bourgeois ideology in the stage of the slow, but inevitable, decay of imperialism, the vacuity of its slogans (can anyone still imagine, as the broad masses were deceived into saying only 15 years ago, that the West is the bulwark of freedom?), and the banal terrorism of its incompetence, were unmasked by revolutionary intellectuals: the victorious struggle of the Vietnamese people revealed the obvious truth of what Mao Zedong had said 20 years earlier: even when armed with the atom bomb, imperialism is a paper tiger.

The leadership of the proletariat's class organization, the PCF had of course lapsed into revisionism and parliamentary cretinism: it was therefore in no state to take the ideological struggle inside the university 'in hand'. But at a distance, the Great Proletarian Cultural Revolution was demonstrating the exceptional power of the radical critique of ideology, reminding us of the simple rigour of the Marxism of class struggle, attaching great importance to the student revolt, unmasking the growing surrender of the Soviet revisionist clique to techno-humanist conformism and to the petty-bourgeois ideology of the 'peaceful road' to socialism, insisting once more that the intellectual labour/manual labour, cities/countryside dichotomies must be dismantled, and putting all its faith in the creative capacities of the masses.

The lightning development of the 'human sciences' was, finally, bringing this disorder to new heights. As we know, these 'disciplines' are no more than techno-police techniques for adapting to the constraints of a class society. They lend the prestige of science to various measures that compensate for inequalities of power (sociology of 'social strata'), the inhumanity of labour relations (so-called industrial sociology), the authoritarian demands of the technical division of labour (educational psychology) . . . But they refute the idea of a sacrosanct difference between the humanities (humanism) and the sciences (technology), and the pompous liturgy that is designed to 'save man' from the threatening 'grip of technology' (or in other words to preserve both the development of the productive forces, capitalist concentration, and the universalising ideology of the 'free' individual and universal suffrage). The human sciences revealed, in a negative sense, the existence – and efficacy – of the authentic theoretical discourses (Marxism and Freudianism), claimed to occupy their terrain and repressed their critical forces. The rebirth of those two sciences took place outside the university (no one has ever been required to sit an examination in Marxism or Freudianism), and the idea of a 'parallel' or 'critical' university was gaining ground; it is true that it was a political absurdity, but it had great mobilizing power. In that respect, the importance, in France, of the seminars of Althusser or Lacan cannot be underestimated; not so much because of their content and the so-called structuralism that was said to dominate them, as because of the practical way in which they demonstrated that the university institution (in the true sense) had fallen into a comfortable rut and was pitifully obedient to its masters. A new apprenticeship in *dogmatic violence*, even if it was dressed somewhat decorously in the rags of Science, served as a form of intellectual training in preparation for the sudden demands of the masses. And besides, without theoretical terrorism, there can be no revolution: ten years – and more – of 'dialogue' had put paid to that vital idea long before the 'structuralists' did so.

The conjunctural set I have just described sheds light on all the student revolts in countries under the hegemony of capitalism. It allows us to point to where overdetermination makes this revolt a real threat to the social order once it goes beyond a certain threshold of violence: 1) Where measures of geographical segregation (the campus) try to isolate and limit the effects of the contradiction, but simply exacerbate its internal effects. 2) Where the 'human sciences' are being developed, even though progressive teachers popularize, deliberately or otherwise, the critique of them. 3) Where the university brings together the broad masses. 4) Where the theme of worker/student unity has an understandable practical significance. 5) Where the university administration is weak, either because its demagogy has no concepts, or because it is authoritarian but powerless. 6) Where groups have been able to establish themselves and actively propagate revolutionary ideological ferment based upon striking and immediately effective practical initiatives.

Nanterre is deployed there.[6]

*

The contradiction first develops in petty-bourgeois milieus, and exacerbates the 'pathological' aspects of Gaullism. This regime, which is bound up with the national tradition of Bonapartism, is attempting to forge a *direct* alliance between the *haute bourgeoisie* (which wields power without any intermediaries: Pompidou and his clique) and classes or social strata that are traditionally unorganized: the peasantry, the parasites in the retail sector, that fraction of the working masses that has been discouraged by the capitulation of the communists but which, in the absence of any ideological support, lapses into economistic spontaneism and the cult of state authority. 'Democratic' demands and

6   The occupation of the university buildings at Nanterre marked the beginning of May '68. *Translator's note.*

hostility to 'personal power', which are the leitmotif
of both social-democrats and revisionists, are used to
voice the discontents of a petty bourgeoisie that has
been excluded from power; while the petty bourgeoisie
still longs for the happy pre-Bonapartist days when it
could bribe the bourgeoisie to legislate in its favour –
and paid a heavy price in terms of anti-communism
and repression – it is gradually moving, despite its
better judgement, in the direction of a politics of
alliance with the proletariat. Its only conception of
that alliance is orderly; it takes, in other words, in the
form of bureaucratic and electoral negotiations. But,
ultimately, it is resigned to it. In 1967, broad masses of
centrist voters voted Communist in the second round
of the elections: this was emblematic of the situation
that, over the last three years, gave rise to a slow and
confused 'Operation Mitterrand'.[7]

This context explains how much is at stake.
The national education system is one of the

7   Having stood unsuccessfully against de Gaulle in 1965,
François Mitterrand tried to position himself in 1968 as the
most appropriate anti-Gaullist candidate in the upcoming
presidential elections. However, in practice in 1969,
Mitterrand was not able to stand. *Translator's note.*

petty bourgeoisie's historic bastions, and the instrument of its hopes of upward social mobility: the mathematical asceticism of the *grandes écoles* gives it access to the business bourgeoisie; studying law or humanities at university gives it access to political prestige. The slogan of 'prioritize national education', the fetishization of schools, and an educational and reformist conception of 'social progress' are the things that bind petty-bourgeois doctrine together. Since 1958, the school system has been the site of the strongest resistance to Bonapartism.

The Gaullist desire to wear down this resistance by making the university the servant of the demands of big capital and by dismantling the institutional (educational) supports that transmit democratic ideology was obvious during the early stages of the crisis: the pauperization and feminization of primary education; the technocratic fragmentation of secondary education, which in other respects was left to respond to the pressure of the masses; draconian selection and strict career guidance in higher education. The 'Fouchet plan', which was too obviously a *dispositif* for this policy, began to meet with stubborn resistance from 1966 onwards, and was then abandoned as the disorder spread.[8]

'The crisis is ripe': the academic year 1967–68 was chaotic and full of incidents. Small but watchful revolutionary groups grew stronger in this contradictory climate. They helped to prevent a fascism that might otherwise have provided an outlet for this petty-bourgeois resentment from taking hold in the student milieu. They put down roots amongst the masses because their anti-imperialist struggles were correct and because they had at least some notion of what Marxism-Leninism meant.

A series of blunders (which had more to do with newspaper headlines than with history) then united not the intelligentsia, which has traditional links with the students, but a broad faction of the bourgeoisie itself, around the well-chosen theme of police repression. Consciously or otherwise – and here we see the superbly creative talents of the masses – the students used all the contradictions'

8   The proposed 'Fouchet reforms' would have introduced strict pre-entry selective criteria for university admissions. *Translator's note.*

resources, and especially the contradiction that prevented the government from further breaking with the petty bourgeoisie by, for example, giving the order to open fire on the masses. That would have been a class *causus belli* and a very different political situation. In that context, the students fought bravely and, by inventing practical methods of struggle (small and fairly well-equipped groups, barricades, calculated insolence), forced the police to take the general line of 'not too far' just 'too far'. When bourgeois public opinion, its press and its broadcasters united against this 'excess', the government had to back down.

The government had, it should be noted, nothing to fear a few months later when young workers in Caen and Redon fought the police with greater violence and obstinacy than the groups in the Latin Quarter ever did. It is therefore wrong to say that the combativeness of the students was the one thing that led to the crisis. Violence does pay, but only when used in the place assigned it by the conjuncture or at the point when the balance of power has been reversed. The crisis arose because an advanced detachment of the petty bourgeoisie (the students) crystallized the built-up resentment around its counter-violence, split state power's class basis and constantly threatened to provoke the *supporting intervention* of the proletariat, which is always quick to take advantage of its historic adversary's helplessness. When, conversely, Gaullism turned on the workers in Caen, Redon and Le Mans, it enjoyed the support, or at least the indifference, of the petty-bourgeois masses, students included. In May, the balance of this triangular configuration, which is the key to class struggle, shifted, and that, at the conceptual level, gave it its revolutionary potential.

This potentiality concerns, *and will always concern*, a mass movement *led by the petty bourgeoisie*. The revolutionary (non-legal) overthrow of the Bonapartist *form* of state power was an objective possibility in May. But the inexistence of a true Marxist–Leninist party has *always* prevented the proletariat from laying claim to the ideological and political leadership of the struggle. The revolutionary overthrow of bourgeois power *as such* has therefore never been possible, or even put on the agenda by the conjuncture, except in the hyper-leftist daydreams, which Lenin described so often, of impassioned and garrulous petty bourgeois. The correct slogan was (and is) 'Long live the democratic-popular revolution'. It is only at a later stage in the struggle, or when it has demonstrated in practice its strength and its political ability to make the slogan a reality, that the proletariat has any claim on the leadership of the movement. Hypotheses, castles in the air.

When there is a real threat that might lead to the fall of a bourgeois *fraction*, the state apparatus's first reaction is to retreat. The specific conditions in which it retreated made its retreat spectacular: what was at stake was clear, and that is an essential point in any trial of strength: it was the 'three conditions' laid down by UNEF [Union National des Etudiants Français – the student union] – and this was an excellent tactical decision that received unwavering support – that made the prime minister Pompidou capitulate. This public demonstration of the effectiveness of activist methods meant that theses that had for years been defended to no avail by small minorities within the workers' movement suddenly became offensive theses. Minorities like the Trotskyist groups in La Voie Ouvrière, the Maoist militants of the UJCML (Union des Jeunesses

Communistes Marxistes-Léninistes), who had links with the productive sector, the anarcho-syndicalists in Force Ouvière, played a decisive role in calling strikes at Sud-Aviation and Renault.

The students' 'victory' and the occupations that followed brought them face to face, however, with some insoluble problems: the problems of how to organize the movement, of its ideological structure, and of its strategic aims. No sooner had it united around the negative and humanist theme of police brutality, which was symbolized by the slogan 'CRS-SS' – a slogan devoid of any real political content – and which it tried to revive whenever the movement began to fragment (as when an attempt was made to revive it with UNEF's 'black book'), than the petty bourgeoisie rediscovered its hostility to the proletarian rigour of scientific socialism, its congenital distrust of class organization, and even of any form of organization, and its emotive individualism, which swung from hyper-revolutionary enthusiasm to deep depression via a melancholic and bad-tempered feeling of having been betrayed.

The defeatist antics of the CGT's bosses dialectically

inspired these inevitable failures, all the more so in that they appeared to justify them. We therefore saw the most astonishing revival of those variants of utopian socialism which, ever since the nineteenth century, have both been the unchanging humus of the French working-class/democratic tradition and a permanent obstacle to the unleashing of Marxism-Leninism's power. Torn between a juridical reformism that fabricated improbable forms of 'autonomy' without any real understanding of the balance of power, and a Blanquist putchism masquerading as urban guerrilla warfare, we imagined that the pathetic actions of a few groups wearing helmets and armed with sticks could bring down the enormous state apparatus (though their courage was never in dispute, which was certainly a new phenomenon). Two names appeared to provide a natural point of equilibrium. The first was that of Proudhon, and it was ignored all the more in that it was, in ideological terms, invoked more widely and more spontaneously; the second was that of Trotsky, who had the support of the activities of the most coherent revolutionary 'Marxist' group, namely the Jeunesse Communiste

Révolutionnaire.[9] The themes of self-management and decentralization came from Proudhon, and that of the omnipotence of the general strike and the pitiless condemnation of 'bureaucracies' from Trotsky. The idea of 'multiple powers' undermined the basic theme of the dictatorship of the proletariat, while correct denunciations of Stalin's errors in fact helped to conceal an individualistic lack of discipline, doctrinal eclecticism and a permanent confusion between revolution and having a good time.

Thanks to an inversion that was far from paradoxical, when the idea of organization did finally come up, it was narrow, aristocratic, 'vanguardist' and military. It took no heed of the masses' demand for organization and for an ideological structure. The uncertainty that is characteristic of the petty bourgeoisie could be seen in the quarrels between the infra-Bolshevism of mass spontaneity, and the hyper-Bolshevism of the intellectual avant-garde. Had it been absolutely preponderant, Mao Zedong's theory of the need for a

---

9   Forerunner of the Ligue Communiste Révolutionnaire – French section of the Fourth International (United Secretariat). *Translator's note.*

mass line could, it is true, have stopped this vacillation. We had yet to reach that stage.

The sudden eruption of the working class will come about thanks to the enchanting din of petty-bourgeois enthusiasms. No one will ever give this formidable but silent shock a form and a voice. The preconditions for practical unity will never be met.

All that remains to be said is that the revolutionary storm was in fact a cyclone that violently swirled around the empty Point, the central void where communist organization was lacking. At a slight remove, we found the enormous, wheezy machine of the Waldeck-Rochets and the Seguys,[10] which perpetuated the lack of organization. This is where militants armed with Mao Zedong Thought should have given form to and led the fight. But we saw only the twitching of 'revisionist clowns', as *Peking News* so aptly put it.

Sad clowns, white clowns. At least the sea of red

---

10   At the time, the General Secretaries of the PCF and the CGT (Confédération Générale du Travail – the Communist-aligned trade union confederation) respectively. *Translator's note*.

flags, which made their lugubrious colours stand out by contrast, swept them – in the eyes of the broad masses – into the gaping dustbins of History, along with their paper masks.

This Crisis Is the Spectacle: Where Is the Real?

The way the global financial crisis is described to us makes it look like one of those big bad films that are concocted by the ready-made hit machine that we now call the 'cinema'. It's all there: the gradual spectacle of the disaster, the crude manipulation of suspense, the exoticism of the identical – the Jakarta stock exchange in the same spectacular boat as New York, the link between Moscow and São Paulo, the same banks going up in the same flames – the terrifying repercussions: ouch, ouch, the best laid 'plans' could not prevent Black Friday, everything is collapsing, everything is going to collapse . . . But there is still hope: the little squad of the powerful has taken centre stage. They are as haggard and as intent on what they are doing as characters in a disaster movie. The Sarkozys, the Paulsons, the Merkels, the Browns, the Trichets – the monetary fire-fighters, pouring billions upon billions into the central Hole. One day we will ask ourselves (this is for future episodes) where they got the money from, because whenever the poor ask for a little something, they've said for years as they turn their pockets out that they haven't got a penny. For the moment, that doesn't matter. 'Save the banks!' That noble, humanist and democratic cry springs from the breast of every politician and all the media. Save them at any price! You've said it! Because none of this comes cheap.

I have to admit it: when I see all these figures circulating – and like almost everyone else, I have no idea what they represent (just what does 400 billion euros look like?) – I trust them. I have every confidence in the fire-fighters. If they all act together, they can do it. I know they can, I can feel it. The banks will be even bigger than before, and a few small and medium-sized banks that initially survived only because they were saved by the benevolence of states will be given to the bigger ones for next to nothing. The collapse of capitalism? You must be joking. And who wants it to collapse anyway? Who even knows what that means, or might mean? Save the banks, I tell you, and everything will turn out well. For the direct actors in the film – the rich, their servants, their parasites, those who envy them and those who sing their praises – a happy ending is inevitable, though it might be a bit melancholy, given the state of the world today and of the policies deployed there.

Let us turn, rather, to those who are watching the show, to the bewildered, slightly worried, crowd. They do not understand much of what is going on and have no active involvement in it. They listen to what sounds like a noise in the distance – the death knell of banks at bay – try imagining the weekends of the glorious little band of government leaders – and it really must be stressful – watch the astronomical figures go by, and automatically compare them with their own resources, and, in the case of a sizeable proportion of humanity, the complete lack of resources that makes the last years of their lives both so bitter and so brave. I am telling you: that is the real, and we will gain access to it only if we take our eyes off the screen and look at the invisible masses of those for whom, until just before they were plunged into something even worse than what they had already experienced, the disaster movie and its schmaltzy ending (Sarko kisses Merkel, and everyone weeps for joy) was never anything more than a shadow play.

There has been a lot of talk recently about the 'real economy' (the production and circulation of goods) and what I suppose has to be called the 'unreal economy', which is supposedly the root of all evil, given that its agents have become 'irresponsible', 'irrational' and 'predatory'. They greedily recycled what had become a shapeless mass of shares, securitizations and money, and then they panicked. The distinction was absurd, and was usually contradicted two lines later by the very different metaphor that described financial circulation and speculation as the 'bloodstream' of the economy. Can the heart and the blood be divorced from the living reality of a body? How can a financial heart attack have no effect on the health of the economy as a whole? Finance capitalism is – and always has been, meaning: for the last 500 years – a central and constituent element of capitalism in general. As for those who own and run this system, their only 'responsibility' is to make a profit. Profit is the measure of their 'rationality'. It is not just that they are predators; it is their duty to be predatory.

So nothing in the baggage hold of capitalist

production could be more 'real' than its commodity store or its speculative compartment. And they corrupt everything else: the vast majority of the objects produced by this type of machinery were only ordered for profit, and for the derivative speculations which generate the fastest and greatest share of those profits. Most of them are ugly, get in the way, and are useless, impractical and useless. And billions have to be spent to convince people that they are not. Which presupposes transforming people into capricious children and eternal adolescents whose lives revolve around getting new toys.

The return to the real is certainly not the path that leads back from a bad and 'irrational' speculation to healthy production. We have to get back to the immediate and reflexive life of all those who live in this world. If we get back to that, we can unflinchingly observe capitalism, and even the disaster movie it has been making us watch. It is not the film that is the real: it is the cinema.

What do we say when we look away, or look back? What do we see when we succeed in ridding ourselves of our slight fear of the void? After all, our masters want us to fear the void, and therefore to beg them to

save the banks. We see, and this is what we call seeing,
simple things that we have known for a long time:
capitalism is nothing but banditry, and it is irrational
in its essence and devastating in its becoming.
Capitalism has always ensured that we pay the price
for a few short decades of brutally inegalitarian
prosperity: crises that swallow up astronomical
quantities of value, bloody punitive expeditions into
all the zones it regards as threatening or strategic,
and the world wars that allow it to recover its health.
That is the dialectical power of an inverted look at the
disaster movie. What? Ignoring the lives of the people
watching the movie, they dare to sing the praises of
a system that hands the organization of our collective
life over to the lowest instincts, to greed, rivalry and
unconscious egotism? They expect us to praise a
'democracy' whose leaders serve the cause of private
financial appropriation so assiduously that they
would astonish Marx himself – Marx who was already
describing governments as 'Capital's executives' 160
years ago? They want at all cost to make ordinary
citizens believe that it is quite impossible to cover
the Social Security deficit, but that we have to cover
the banks' deficit, no matter how many billons it

costs us. We must sagely nod our heads when no one even thinks of nationalizing a factory that runs into difficulty because of the competition, even though thousands of people work there, while agreeing that obviously we have to nationalize banks that have gone bust thanks to their speculative activities.

The real, in this context, is clearly that which existed before the crisis. Where did this entire financial phantasmagoria come from? Quite simply from the way people who could just not afford them were forced into buying nice new houses because they were seduced into taking out miraculous loans. Their promises to repay the loans were then sold on, after having been mixed up with securitizations whose composition had, like that of designer drugs, been made as clever as it was opaque thanks to the work of battalions of mathematicians. They were bought and sold on, and all this money circulated, and increased in value when its was invested in far-away banks. Yes, all this money in circulation was secured against real houses. But then the property market collapsed, and that was all it took to ensure the buyers were less and less able to pay their debts, because their houses were worth less, while their creditors were demanding more. And when they could not pay anything at all, the drugs that had been injected into securitizations poisoned them: they were no longer worth anything. It looked like a draw: the speculators lost their stake money and the buyers lost their homes when they were gently evicted. But, as always, it was the collective dimension and ordinary life that lost out. Ultimately, all this came about because tens of millions of people are on such low incomes – or non-incomes – that they cannot afford anywhere to live. The real essence of the financial crisis is a housing crisis. And the people who cannot afford anywhere to live are certainly not bankers. We have to go back to the lives of ordinary people.

The only desirable outcome of all this is the hope that the real will still be what it was before the crisis, in so far as that is possible. And that the lessons to be learned from this whole sorry business are learned by peoples, not by bankers, the governments that serve them, and the newspapers that serve governments.

In my view, this return of the real is articulated at two levels. The first is obviously political. Given that, as the film demonstrates, 'democratic' politics means nothing more than an eager willingness to service the needs of the banks, its real name is 'capitalo-parliamentarianism'. We must, as many experiments have tried to do over the past 20 years, organize a very different kind of politics. That politics is far removed from state power, and will probably remain so for a long time to come, but that is of no import. It begins at the level of the real, with a practical alliance with those people who are in the best position to invent it in the immediate: the new proletarians who have come from Africa and elsewhere, and the intellectuals who are the heirs to the political battles of recent decades. The alliance will gradually expand, depending on what they are able to achieve. It will not have any organic relationship with existing parties or the electoral and institutional system that sustains them. It will invent the new discipline of those who have nothing, their political capacities, and a new idea of what their victory might mean.

The second level is ideological. We have to overturn the old verdict that would have us believe we are living in the age of the 'end of ideologies'. We can now see quite clearly that the only reality behind their so-called 'end' is 'Save the banks'. Nothing could be more important than rediscovering the passion for ideas,

or than contrasting the world as it is with a general
hypothesis, with the certainty that we can create a very
different order of things. We will contrast the wicked
spectacle of capitalism with the real of peoples,
with the lives of people and the movement of ideas.
The theme of the emancipation of humanity has lost
none of its power. Of course the word 'communism',
which was for a long time the name of that power, has
been cheapened and prostituted. But if we allow it to
disappear, we surrender to the supporters of order, to
the febrile actors in the disaster movie. We are going
to resuscitate that name in all its new clarity. Which
was also its old virtue, as it was when Marx said of
communism that it '*involves the most radical rupture
with traditional associations*' and will give rise to '*an
association, in which the free development of each is the
condition for the free development of all.*'

A radical rupture with capitalo-parliamentarianism,
a politics invented at the grassroots level of the popular
real, and the sovereignty of the idea: it is all there, and
it will distract us from the disaster movie and remind
us of our uprising.

II

The Cultural Revolution:
The Last Revolution?[1]

Why?

W hy discuss the 'Cultural Revolution', the official name for a long period of serious disturbances in Communist China between 1965 and 1976? For at least three reasons:

1. The Cultural Revolution has been a constant and lively point of reference for militant activity throughout the world, and particularly in France, at least between 1967 and 1976. It is part of our political history and the basis for the existence of the Maoist current, the only true political creation of the sixties and seventies. I can say 'our', for I was part of it, and in a certain sense,

---

1   From the second conference in the Rouge Gorge series, delivered by Alain Badiou in February 2002 at the Maison des écrivains in Paris. *Translator's note.*

to quote Rimbaud, 'I am there, I am still there.' In the untiring inventiveness of the Chinese revolutionaries, all sorts of subjective and practical trajectories have found their justification – to change subjectivity, to live otherwise, to think otherwise: the Chinese – and then we – called that 'revolutionization'. Their aim: 'To change the human being in what is most profound.' They taught that in political practice, we must be both 'the arrow and the bull's eye', because the old worldview is also still present within us. By the end of the sixties, we were present everywhere: in the factories, in the suburbs, in the countryside. Tens of thousands of students became proletarian or went to live among the workers. For this too we had the phrases of the Cultural Revolution: the 'great exchanges of experience', 'to serve the people', and, always the essential slogan: the 'mass alliance'. We fought against the brutal inertia of the PCF (Parti Communiste Français), against its violent conservatism. In China too the party bureaucracy was attacked; that was called 'the struggle against revisionism'. Even the splits, the confrontations between revolutionaries from different orientations, were referred to in the Chinese manner: 'to hunt down the black gangsters', ending with those who are 'leftist in appearance and rightist

in reality'. When we came across a popular political
situation, a factory strike or a confrontation with the
fascistic landlords, we knew that we had 'to excel in
the discovery of the proletarian left, to rally the centre,
to isolate and crush the right'. Mao's *Little Red Book*
has been our guide, not, as fools say, in the service of
a dogmatic catechism, but on the contrary, so that we
can clarify and invent new behaviours in all sorts of
disparate situations that were unfamiliar to us. With
regard to all this, since I am not one of those who justify
their abandonment and their rallying to the established
reaction with references to the psychology of illusions
or to blind morality, we can only quote our sources, and
pay homage to the Chinese revolutionaries.

2. The Cultural Revolution is the typical example
(yet another notion from Maoism, the typical example:
a revolutionary discovery that must be generalized) of
a political experience that saturates the form of the
party-state. I use the term 'saturation' in the sense
given to it by Sylvain Lazarus;[2] I will attempt to show
that the Cultural Revolution is the last significant
political sequence that is still internal to the party-state

2   Sylvain Lazarus, *Anthropologie du nom*, Seuil, 1996, p. 37.

(in this case, the Chinese Communist Party), and fails as such. But May 1968 and its aftermath, that is slightly different. The Polish movement or Chiapas, that is very different. The Organisation Politique, that is absolutely different. But without the saturation of the sixties and seventies, nothing would as yet be thinkable, outside the spectre of the party-state, or the parties-state.[3]

3. The Cultural Revolution is a great lesson in history and politics, in history as thought from within politics (and not the other way around). Indeed, depending on whether we examine this 'revolution' (the word itself lies at the heart of the saturation) according to the dominant historiography or according to a real political question, we arrive at striking disagreements. What matters is for us to see clearly that the nature of this discord is not of the order of empirical or positivist precision or lack thereof. We can be in agreement as to the facts, and end up with judgements that are perfectly

3 On the party-state or parties-state as central figures of politics in the twentieth century, see the previous conference in the series of Rouge Gorge, *Les trois régimes du sícle*, presented by Sylvain Lazarus (2001).

opposed to one another. It is precisely this paradox that will serve as our point of entry into the subject matter.

Narratives

The dominant historiographical version was compiled by various specialists, especially by Sinologists, as early as 1968, and it has not changed since then. It was consolidated by the fact that covertly it became the official version of a Chinese state dominated after 1976 by people who escaped from and sought revenge for the Cultural Revolution, headed by Deng Xiaoping.

What does this version say?[4] It says that, in terms of revolution, it was a matter of a power struggle at the top echelons of the bureaucracy of the party-state. That Mao's economic voluntarism, incarnated in the call

---

4   A book that gives an idea of the general style of the official and 'critical' versions (for once, these strangely agree) of the Cultural Revolution is that by Simon Leys [i.e. Pierre Ryckmans], *The Chairman's New Clothes: Mao and the Cultural Revolution*, trans. Carol Appleyard and Patrick Goode, Schocken Books, 1981.

for 'the Great Leap Forward', was a complete failure, leading to the return of famine to the countryside. That following this failure, Mao finds himself in the minority among the leading party authorities, and that a 'pragmatic' group imposes its law, the dominant personalities of which are Liu Shaoqi (then named president of the Republic), Deng Xiaoping (general secretary of the Party) and Peng Zhen (mayor of Beijing). That, as early as 1963, Mao attempted to lead some counter-attacks, but that he failed among the regular party authorities. That he then had recourse to forces foreign to the party, whether external (the student Red Guards) or external/internal, particularly the army, over which he took control again after the elimination of Peng Dehuai and his replacement by Lin Biao.[5] That then, solely because of Mao's will to regain power, there ensued a bloody and chaotic situation, which persisted until the death of the culprit (in 1976).

It is totally feasible to accept that nothing in this

---

5   With regard to these episodes, and more generally the principal facts of the period, see the chronology included at the end of this chapter.

version is properly speaking incorrect. But its real meaning can emerge only from a political understanding of the events, that is, their concentration in a form of thinking still active today.

1. No stabilization? True. But that is because it turned out to be impossible to develop the political innovation within the framework of the party-state. Neither the most extensive creative freedom of the student and working masses (between 1966 and 1968) nor the ideological and state control of the army (between 1968 and 1971), nor the ad hoc solutions to the problems isssued in a Politburo dominated by the confrontation among antagonistic tendencies (between 1972 and 1976) allowed the revolutionary ideas to take root so that an entirely new political situation, completely detached from the Soviet model, could finally see the light of day on the scale of society as a whole.

2. Recourse to external forces? True. But this was intended, and it actually had the effect, both on a short-term and on a long-term basis, perhaps even until today, of partly disentangling party and state. It was a matter of destroying bureaucratic formalism, at least for the duration of a massive movement. The

fact that this provoked the anarchy of factions at the same time signals an essential political question for times to come: what gives unity to a politics, if it is not directly guaranteed by the formal unity of the state?

3. A struggle for power? Of course. It is rather ridiculous to oppose 'power struggle' and 'revolution' since by 'revolution' we can only understand the articulation of antagonistic political forces over the question of power. Besides, the Maoists constantly quoted Lenin, for whom the question of the revolution in the final instance is explicitly that of power. Rather, the real problem, which is very complex, would be to know whether the Cultural Revolution does not in fact put an end to the revolutionary conception of the articulation between politics and the state. Indeed, this was its great question, its central and violent debate.

4. The 'Great Leap Forward' – a cruel failure? Yes, in many respects. But this failure is the result of a critical examination of Stalin's economic doctrine. It can certainly not be attributed to a uniform treatment of questions related to the development of the countryside by 'totalitarianism'. Mao severely

examined (as witnessed by numerous written notes) the Stalinist conception of collectivization and its absolute disdain for the peasants. His idea was certainly not to collectivize through force and violence in order to ensure accumulation at all costs in the cities. It was, quite the contrary, to industrialize the countryside locally, to give it a relative economic autonomy, in order to avoid the savage proletarianization and urbanization that had taken a catastrophic shape in the USSR. In truth, Mao followed the communist idea of an effective resolution of the contradiction between city and countryside, and not that of a violent destruction of the countryside in favour of the cities. If there is a failure, it is of a political nature, and it is a completely different failure from Stalin's. Ultimately, we should affirm that the same abstract description of facts by no means leads to the same mode of thinking when it operates under different political axioms.

Dates

The quarrel is equally clear when it comes to dates. The dominant point of view, which is also that of the Chinese State, is that the Cultural Revolution lasted for ten years, from 1966 to 1976, from the Red Guards to Mao's death. Ten years of troubles, ten years lost for a rational development.

In fact, this dating can be defended, if one reasons from the strict point of view of the history of the Chinese State, with the following criteria: civil stability, production, a certain unity at the head of the administration, cohesion in the army, etc. But this is not my axiom and these are not my criteria. If one examines the question of dates from the point of view of politics, of political invention, the principal criteria become the following: when can we say that there is a situation of collective creations of thought of the political type? When does practice with its directives stand in a verifiable excess over the tradition and function of the Chinese party-state? When do statements of universal value emerge? Then, we proceed in a completely different way to determine the boundaries of the process named the 'Great Proletarian Cultural Revolution', which we among ourselves called 'the GPCR'.

As far as I am concerned, I propose that the Cultural Revolution, in this conception, forms a sequence that runs from November 1965 to July 1968. I can even accept (this is a matter of political technique) a drastic reduction, which would situate the revolutionary moment properly speaking between May 1966 and September 1967. The criterion is the existence of a political activity of the masses, its slogans, its new organizations, its own places. Through all of this an ambivalent but undeniable reference is constituted for all contemporary political thought worthy of the name. In this sense, there is 'revolution' because there are the Red Guards, the revolutionary rebel workers, innumerable organizations and 'general headquarters', totally unpredictable situations, new political statements, texts without precedent, etc.

Hypothesis

How to proceed so that this gigantic upheaval is exposed to thought and makes sense today? I will formulate a hypothesis and experiment on several levels, both factual and textual, of the sequence I am referring to (that is, China between November 1965 and July 1968).

The hypothesis is the following: We are in the conditions of an essential division of the party-state (the

Chinese Communist Party, in power since 1949). This division is essential in that it entails crucial questions regarding the future of the country: the economy and the relation between city and countryside; the eventual transformation of the army; the assessment of the Korean War; the intellectuals, universities, art and literature; and, finally, the value of the Soviet, or Stalinist, model. But it is also and above all essential because the minority trend among the party cadres is at the same time led, or represented, by the person whose historical and popular legitimacy is the greatest, that is, Mao Zedong. There is a formidable phenomenon of non-coincidence between the historicity of the party (the long period of the popular war, first against the Japanese, then against Chiang Kai-shek) and the present state of its activity as the framework of state power. Moreover, the Yanan period will be constantly invoked during the Cultural Revolution, particularly in the army, as a model of communist political subjectivity.

This phenomenon has the following consequences: the confrontation between positions cannot be ruled by bureaucratic formalism, but neither can it be ruled by the methods of terrorist purging that Stalin used in the thirties. In the space of the party-state, though, there is only formalism or terror. Mao and his group will have to invent a third recourse, a recourse to political mass mobilization, to try to break with the representatives of the majority trend and, in particular, their leaders at the upper echelons of the party and the state. This recourse assumes that one admit uncontrolled forms of revolt and organization. Mao's group, after a great deal of hesitation, will in fact impose that these be admitted, first in the universities and then in the factories. But, in a contradictory move, it will also try to bring together all organizational innovations of the revolution in the general space of the party-state.

Here we are at the heart of the hypothesis: the Cultural Revolution is the historical development of a contradiction. On one hand, the issue is to arouse mass revolutionary action in the margins of the state of the dictatorship of the proletariat, or to acknowledge, in the theoretical jargon of the time, that even though the state is formally a 'proletarian' state, the class struggle continues, including forms of mass revolt. Mao and his followers will go so far as to say that under socialism, the bourgeoisie reconstitutes itself and organizes itself *within the Communist Party itself.* On the other hand, with actual civil war still being excluded, the general form of the relation between the party and the state, in particular concerning the use of repressive forces, must remain unchanged at least in so far as it is not really a question of *destroying* the party. Mao will make this known by noting that 'the overwhelming majority of cadres are good'.

This contradiction will at the same time produce a succession of instances of local revolt that exceed the party's authority, the violent anarchy of these excesses, the inevitability of a call to order of extraordinary brutality, and, in the end, the decisive entrance on to the stage of the people's army.

These successive excesses establish the chronology (the stages) of the Cultural Revolution. The leading revolutionary group will first try to keep the revolt within the context of the educational institutions. This attempt began to fail in August 1966, when the Red Guards spread throughout the cities. Afterwards, it will be a question of containing the revolt within the framework of youth in school and university. But from the end of 1966 and particularly from January 1967 onward, workers become the principal force of the movement. Then the quest is on to keep the party and state administrations at a distance, but they will be in the midst of the turmoil starting in 1967 through a series of power struggles. Finally, the aim will be to keep the army in check at any cost as a power in reserve, a last resource. But this will turn out to be almost impossible with the unleashing of violence in August 1967 in Wuhan and Canton. It is precisely with an eye on the real risk of a schism among the armed forces that the slow movement of repressive inversion will set in, beginning in September 1967.

Let us put it like this: the political innovations which gave the sequence its unquestionable revolutionary appeal could not be deployed except in so far as they exceeded the aim assigned to them by those whom the actors of the revolution themselves (the youth and its innumerable groups, the rebel workers . . .) considered to be their natural leaders: Mao and his minority group. By the same token, these innovations have always been localized and particular; they could not really turn into strategic and reproducible propositions. In the end, the strategic meaning (or the universal range) of these innovations was negative.

Because what they themselves meant, and what they strongly impressed upon the militant minds of the entire world, was nothing but the end of the party-state as the central product of revolutionary political activity. More generally, the Cultural Revolution showed that it was no longer possible to submit either the revolutionary mass actions or the organizational phenomena to the strict logic of class representation. That is why it remains a political episode of the highest importance.

Experimental fields

I would like to experiment with the above hypothesis by testing it according to seven referents, taken in chronological order:

1. The 'Sixteen Points' decision of August 1966, which is probably for the most part from the hand of Mao himself, and which in any case is the most innovative central document, the one that breaks most abruptly with the bureaucratic formalism of parties-state.

2. The Red Guards and Chinese society (in the period from August 1966 to at least August 1967).

Without a doubt, this involves an exploration of the limits of the political capacity of high-school and university students left more or less to themselves, whatever the circumstances.

3. The 'revolutionary rebel workers' and the Shanghai Commune (January/February 1967), a major and unfinished episode, because it proposes an alternative form of power to the centralism of the party.

4. The power seizures: the 'great alliance', 'triple combination', and 'revolutionary committees', from January 1967 to the spring of 1968. Here the question is whether the movement really creates new organizations, or whether it amounts only to a regeneration of the party.

5. The Wuhan incident (July 1967). Here we are at the peak of the movement: the army risks division, and the far left pushes its advantage, but only to succumb.

6. The workers' entry into the universities (end of July 1968), which is in reality the final episode of the existence of independent student organizations.

7. Mao's cult of personality. This feature has so often been the object of sarcasm in the West that in the end we have forgotten to ask ourselves what meaning it might well have had, and in particular,

what its meaning is within the Cultural Revolution, where the 'cult' functioned as a flag, not for the party conservatives, but for worker and student rebels.

The Decision in Sixteen Points

This text was adopted at a session of the Central Committee on 8 August 1966. With a certain genius it presents the fundamental contradiction of the endeavour called the 'Cultural Revolution'. One sign of this presentation is of course the fact that the text does not explain, or barely explains, the name ('cultural') relating to the ongoing political sequence, except for the enigmatic and metaphysical first sentence: 'The Cultural Revolution seeks to change people in what is most profound.'[6] Here,

6 Badiou, as is often the case, does not give textual references here, but elsewhere in his work, when dealing with the Cultural Revolution, he tends to quote from the French translations included in another 'little red book' that also seems to be his source here: *La Grande Révolution Culturelle Prolétarienne: Recueil de documents importants*, Beijing: Editions en langues étrangères, 1970. In English, the corresponding line of the 'Sixteen Points' sounds even more metaphysical: 'The Great Proletarian Cultural Revolution now unfolding is a great revolution that touches people to their

'cultural' is equivalent to 'ideological', in a particularly radical sense.

A whole portion of the text is a pure and simple call for free revolt, in the great tradition of revolutionary legitimizations.

The text is quite probably illegal, as the composition of the Central Committee was 'corrected' by Mao's group with the support of the army (or certain units loyal to Lin Biao). Revolutionary militants from the university are present, while conservative bureaucrats have been prevented from taking part. In reality, and this is very important, this decision begins a long period of non-existence both of the Central Committee and of the party's secretariat. The important central texts from now on will be signed conjointly by four institutions: the Central Committee, certainly, but which is now only a phantom; the 'Cultural Revolution Group', a highly restricted ad hoc group,[7] which

---

very souls', in *The Chinese Cultural Revolution*, ed. K. H. Fan, Monthly Review Press, 1968, p. 162. All subsequent quotations in the text are from this edition. *Translator's note.*
7   Until September 1967, the leading Maoist group comprises a dozen persons: Mao, Lin Biao, Chen Boda, Jiang Qing, Yao Wenyuan, Zhou Enlai, Kang Sheng, Zhang

nonetheless dispenses of the real political power
properly speaking in so far as it is recognized by
the rebels; the State Council, presided over by Zhou
Enlai; and, finally, as the guarantee of a minimum
of administrative continuity, the formidable Military
Commission of the Central Committee, restructured
by Lin Biao.

Certain passages of the circular are particularly
virulent, concerning both the immediate revolutionary
requirement and the need to oppose the party with
new forms of organization.

Concerning popular mobilization, we will cite in
particular points 3 and 4, entitled 'Put Daring Above
Everything Else and Boldly Arouse the Masses' and
'Let the Masses Educate Themselves in the Movement'.
For example:

Chunqiao, Wang Li, Guan Feng, Lin Jie, Qi Benyu. Chen Yi,
an old centre-right veteran and courageous humourist, is said
to have asked: 'Is that it, the great Chinese Communist Party?
Twelve persons?' We could nonetheless note that the leading
group of the Committee of Public Safety between 1792 and
1794 was far more restricted. Revolutions combine gigantic
mass movements with an often very restricted political
leadership.

What the Central Committee of the Party demands of the Party committees at all levels is that they persevere in giving correct leadership, put daring above everything else, boldly arouse the masses, change the state of weakness and incompetence where it exists, encourage those comrades who have made mistakes but are willing to correct them to cast off their mental burdens and join in the struggle, and dismiss from their leading posts all those in authority who are taking the capitalist road and so make possible the recapture of the leadership for the proletarian revolutionaries.

Or, again:

Trust the masses, rely on them and respect their initiative. Cast out fear. Don't be afraid of disturbances. Chairman Mao has often told us that revolution cannot be so very refined, so gentle, so temperate, kind, courteous, restrained and magnanimous. Let the masses educate themselves in this great revolutionary movement and learn to distinguish between right and wrong and between correct and incorrect ways of doing things.

One detail of point 7 is particularly important and will have immense practical consequences. Here it is:

> no measure should be taken against students at universities, colleges, middle schools, and primary schools because of problems that arise in the movement.

Everybody in China understands that, at least for the period that is now beginning, the revolutionary youth in the cities is guaranteed a form of impunity. It is evident that this is what will allow the youth to spread through the country, parading the revolutionary spirit, in any case until September 1967.

Concerning the forms of organization, point 9, entitled 'Cultural Revolutionary Groups, Committees, and Congresses', sanctions the invention, within and by the movement, of multiple political regroupings outside the party:

> Many new things have begun to emerge in the Great Proletarian Cultural Revolution. The cultural revolutionary groups, committees, and other organizational forms created by the masses

in many schools and units are something new and of great historic importance.

These new organizations are not considered temporary, which proves that the Maoist group, in August of 1966, envisions the destruction of the political monopoly of the party:

Therefore, the cultural revolutionary groups, committees and congresses should not be temporary organizations but permanent, standing mass organizations.

In the end, we are clearly dealing with organizations that are subject to mass democracy, and not to party authority, as shown by the reference to the Paris Commune, that is, to a proletarian situation previous to the Leninist theory of the party:

It is necessary to institute a system of general elections, like that of the Paris Commune, for electing the members to the cultural revolutionary groups and committees and delegates to the cultural revolutionary congresses. The lists

of candidates should be put forward by the
revolutionary masses after full discussion, and
the elections should be held after the masses
have discussed the lists over and over again.

If these members or delegates prove
incompetent, they can be replaced through
election or recalled by the masses after
discussion.

However, if we read the text carefully, knowing what it
means 'to read a text' when it comes from the leadership
of a communist party, we observe that, through crucial
restrictions on the freedom of criticism, some kind of
lock is put on the revolutionary impulse to which the
text constantly appeals.

First of all, it is held, as if axiomatically, that in
essence the party is good. Point 8 ('The Question of
Cadres') distinguishes four types of cadres, as put to
the test of the Cultural Revolution (let us remember
that in China, a 'cadre' is anyone who dispenses
authority, even if minimal): good, comparatively good,
those who have made serious mistakes that can be
fixed, and lastly 'the small number of anti-Party and
anti-socialist Rightists'. The thesis is then that 'the

first two categories (good and comparatively good) are the great majority'. That is, the state apparatus and its internal leadership (the party) are essentially in good hands, which renders paradoxical the recourse to such large-scale revolutionary methods.

Secondly, even if it is said that the masses must take the initiative, the explicit criticism by name of those responsible for the state or the party is in fact severely controlled 'from above'. On this point, the hierarchical structure of the party makes a sudden comeback (point 11, 'The Question of Criticizing by Name in the Press'):

Criticism of anyone by name in the press should be decided after discussion by the Party committee at the same level, and in some cases submitted to the Party committee at a higher level for approval.

The result of this directive will be that innumerable cadres of the party, to begin with the president of the Republic, Liu Shaoqi, will be violently criticized for months, even years, by mass revolutionary organizations in the 'small journals', cartoons, mural posters, before their name appears in the central press. But, at the same time, these criticisms will keep a local character, or be open to annulment. They will leave in the air what *decisions* correspond to them.

Point 15, 'The Armed Forces', finally, which is extremely succinct, raises a decisive question as if in a void: Who has authority over the repressive apparatus? Classically, Marxism indicates that a revolution must break down the repressive apparatus of the state it aims to transform from top to bottom. That is certainly not what is understood in this case:

> In the armed forces, the Cultural Revolution and the socialist education movement should be carried out in accordance with the instructions of the Military Commission of the Central Committee of the Party and the General Political Department of the People's Liberation Army. Here again, we come back to the centralized authority of the party.

Ultimately, the Decision in Sixteen Points combines approaches that are still heterogeneous, and, because of its war-like appeal, it prepares the successive impasses of the movement in its relation to the party-state. Of course, there is always the question of how to define, on the basis of the mass movement, a political path that would be different from the one imposed during previous years by the principal current among the party leadership. But two essential questions remain unsolved: who designates the enemies, who sets the targets of revolutionary criticism? And what is, in this sombre affair, the role of the considerable repressive apparatus: public security, militias and army?

Red Guards and Chinese Society

Following on the heels of the August circular, the phenomenon of the 'Red Guards', organizations of high-school students, will take on extraordinary significance. We know of the gigantic meetings at Tiananmen, which carry on until the end of 1966, where Mao shows himself, mute, to hundreds of thousands of young men and women. But the most important point is that revolutionary organizations storm the cities, using trucks lent by the army, and then the rest of the country, taking advantage of the free train transportation according to the programme of 'exchange of experiences'.

It is clear that what we have here is the strike force behind the movement's extension to the whole of China. Within this movement an absolutely amazing freedom reigns; groups openly confront each other, the journals, tracts, banners and never-ending mural posters reproduce revelations of all kinds along with the political declarations. Fierce caricatures spare almost no one (in August of 1967, the questioning of Zhou Enlai in one of the great mural posters put up overnight will be one of the reasons for the fall of the so-called 'ultra-leftist' tendency). Processions with gongs, drums and loud proclamations take place until late at night.

On the other hand, the tendency towards militarization and uncontrolled action by shock groups soon makes its appearance. The general slogan speaks of a revolutionary struggle against old ideas and old customs (that is what gives content to the adjective 'cultural', which in Chinese means rather 'civilizational' and, in old Marxist jargon, 'superstructural'. Many groups gave this slogan a destructive and violent, even persecutory, interpretation. The hunting-down of women wearing braids, of formally educated intellectuals, of hesitant professors, of all the 'cadres' who do not use the same phraseology as such-and-such a splinter group, the raiding of libraries or museums, the unbearable arrogance of small revolutionary chiefs with regard to the mass of the undecided – all that will soon provoke a genuine revulsion among ordinary people against the extremist wing of the Red Guards.

At bottom, the problem had already been raised in the communiqué of 16 May 1966, Mao's first public act of rebellion against the majority of the Central Committee. This communiqué bluntly declares the need to contend that 'without destruction, there is no construction'. It stigmatizes the conservatives, who preach the 'constructive' spirit to oppose any destruction of the basis of their power. But the balance is hard to find between the evidence of destruction and the slow and tortuous character of construction.

The truth is that, armed only with the slogan of 'the fight of the new against the old', many Red Guards gave in to a well-known (negative) tendency in revolutions: iconoclasm, the persecution of people for futile motives, a sort of assumed barbarism. This is also an inclination of youth left to its own devices. From this we will draw the conclusion that every political organization must be transgenerational, and that it is a bad idea to organize the political separation of youth.

For sure, the Red Guards in no way invent the anti-intellectual radicalism of the revolutionary spirit. At the moment of pronouncing the death sentence of the chemist Lavoisier during the French Revolution, the public accuser Fouquier-Tinville offered this remarkable statement: 'The Republic has no need for scientists.' What happens is that a true revolution considers that it has itself created everything it needs, and we should respect this creative absolutism. In this regard the Cultural Revolution was a true revolution. On the question of science and technology, the fundamental slogan was that what matters is to be 'red', not to be an 'expert'. Or, in the 'moderate' version, which would become the official one: one must be 'red and expert', but red above all.

However, what made the barbarism of certain revolutionary shock groups considerably worse was the fact that there was never, in the sphere of youth action, a global political space for political affirmation, for the positive creation of the new. The tasks of criticism and of destruction had a self-evidence to them that was lacking in the tasks of invention, and all the more so as the latter remained tied to the relentless struggles going on at the top levels of the state.

The Shanghai Commune

The end of 1966 and the beginning of 1967 represent an important moment of the Cultural Revolution with the massive and decisive appearance on the scene by the factory workers. Shanghai plays a pilot role during this important time.

We should consider the paradox inherent in this appearance on the scene of those who officially constitute the 'leading class' of the Chinese State. This comes about, if I may say so, from the Right. In December 1966, indeed, it is the local bureaucrats, the conservative leadership of the party and the municipality who use a working-class contingent – most notably the trade unionists – against the Maoist movement of the Red Guards. Not unlike the way, I might add, in which in France, in May 1968 and the years to follow, the PCF attempted to use the old guard of the CGT (Conseil Générale du Travail) against the revolutionary students who were allied with young workers. Taking advantage of a changing situation, the bosses of the party and municipality of Shanghai launch the workers on the path of all kinds of sectoral demands of a purely economic nature, and in so doing set them up against any intervention coming from the young revolutionaries in the factories and in the administrations (just as in May 1968, the PCF put up a barricade around the factories with picket-lines drawn from its employees, and everywhere hunted down the 'leftists'). Using violent tactics, these unionized movements become quite sizeable, especially the strikes of the transportation and energy sectors, which seek to foster an atmosphere of chaos so that the party bosses can present themselves as the saviours of order. For all these reasons, the revolutionary minority will be forced to intervene against the bureaucratized strikes and to oppose the 'economism' and the demand for 'material incentives' with an austere campaign in favour of communist work and, above all, for the primacy of global political consciousness over and above particular demands.

This will be the backdrop for the great slogan supported in particular by Lin Biao: 'Fight against egoism and criticize revisionism' (we know that 'revisionist' for the Maoists designates abandoning all revolutionary dynamics followed by the USSR, by the communist parties that depend on it, and by a large number of cadres from the Chinese Party).

In the beginning, the Maoist workers' group is rather weak. There is talk of 4,000 workers by the end of 1966. It is true that this group will link itself to the Red Guards and constitute an activist minority. But this does not take away the fact that its field of action in the factories properly speaking is not very large, except in certain machine-tool factories. That was their great claim to fame, and their example would be invoked by revolutionaries for several years to come. In my opinion, it is indeed because the direct action of the workers in the factories comes up against very lively resistance (the bureaucracy has its stronghold there) that the Maoist activists will begin to deploy themselves on the scale of an urban power. With aid from a segment of the cadres who have been loyal to Mao for a long time, as well as from a fraction of the army, they will purge the municipality and the

local party committee. Hence what will be called
the 'seizure of power', which under the name of the
'Shanghai Commune' will mark a turning point in the
Cultural Revolution.

This seizure of power is immediately paradoxical.
On the one hand, like the Decision in Sixteen Points
above, it finds inspiration in a complete counter-model
of the party-state: the coalition of the most disparate
organizations that constituted the Paris Commune and
whose ineffective anarchy had already been criticized
by Marx. On the other hand, this counter-model has
no possibility of national development in so far as on
the national level the figure of the party remains the
only one allowed, even if a number of its traditional
elements are in crisis. Throughout the tumultuous
episodes of the revolution, Zhou Enlai has remained
the guarantee of the unity of the state and of a minimal
level of functionality of the administration. As far as
we know, he was never disavowed by Mao in this task,
which forced him to navigate as closely as possible,
including as closely as possible to the right-wing
elements (it is he who will put Deng Xiaoping back in
the saddle, 'the second highest in power of those who,
despite being in the party, are taking the capitalist

road', to use the revolutionary phrase, and this from the middle of the 1970s onwards). Zhou Enlai, however, made it very clear to the Red Guards that if the 'exchanges of experience' in the entire country were admissible, no revolutionary organization of national importance could be allowed.

Thus the Shanghai Commune, drawn after endless discussions from local student and worker organizations, can attain only a fragile unity. Here again, if the gesture is fundamental (the 'seizure of power' by the revolutionaries), its political space is too narrow. As a result, the workers' entry on to the scene marks both and at the same time a spectacular broadening of the revolutionary mass base, a gigantic and sometimes violent test of bureaucratized forms of power, and the short-lived outline of a new articulation between the popular political initiative and the power of the state.

The power seizures

During the first months of 1967, following the lesson of the events in Shanghai where the revolutionaries have overthrown the anti-Maoist municipality, we will see 'seizures of power' proliferate throughout the country. There is a striking material aspect to this movement: the revolutionaries, organized in small splinter and battle groups essentially made up of students and workers, invade all kinds of administrative offices, including those of the municipalities or the party, and, generally in a Dionysian confusion that is not without violence and destruction, they install a new 'power' in them. Frequently, the old guards who resist are 'shown to the masses', which is not a peaceful ceremony. The bureaucrat, or the presumed bureaucrat, carries a dunce's cap and a sign describing his crimes; he must lower his head, and receive some kicks, or worse. These exorcisms are otherwise well-known revolutionary practices. It is a matter of letting the gathering of ordinary people know that the old untouchables, those whose insolence was silently accepted, are themselves from now on given over to public humiliation. After their victory in 1949, the Chinese communists organized ceremonies of this kind everywhere in the countryside, in order morally to criticize the old large landowners, the 'local despots and evil tyrants', making it known to the smallest Chinese peasants, who for centuries counted for nothing, that the world had 'risen on new foundations' and that from now on they were to be the true masters of the country.

However, we should note that, from February onwards, the 'commune' disappears as the term by which to designate the new local powers, only to be replaced by the expression 'revolutionary committee'. This change is by no means insignificant, because 'committee' has always been the name for the provincial or municipal party organs. We will thus see a vast movement to install new 'revolutionary committees' in all the provinces. And it is not at all clear if these reduplicate, or purely and simply replace, the old and dreaded 'party committees'.

In fact, the ambiguity of the name designates the committee as the impure product of the political conflict. For the local revolutionaries, it is a matter of substituting a different political power for the party, after the nearly complete elimination of the old leading cadres. For the conservatives, who defend themselves at every step, it is a matter of putting back in place the local cadres after the mere fiction of a critique. They are encouraged along this path by the repeated declarations from the Central

Committee about the good nature of the vast majority of party cadres. For the Maoist national leadership, concentrated in the very small 'Central Committee's Cultural Revolution Group', a dozen persons, it is a matter of defining the stakes for the revolutionary organizations (the 'seizing of power') and of inspiring a lasting fear in their adversaries, all the while preserving the general framework for the exercise of power, which remains in their eyes the party and the party alone.

The formulas that are gradually put forward will privilege unity. There will be talk of a 'triple combination', which means: to unify in the committees one-third of newly arrived revolutionaries, one-third of old cadres having accomplished their self-criticism, and one-third of military personnel. There will be talk of a 'great alliance', meaning that locally the revolutionary organizations are asked to unite among themselves and to stop the confrontations (sometimes armed ones). This unity in fact implies a growing amount of coercion, including with regard to the content of the discussions, as well as an increasingly severe limitation of the right to organize freely around one initiative or conviction or another. But how could it be otherwise, except by letting the situation drift into civil war, and by leaving the outcome in the hands of the repressive apparatus? This debate will occupy almost the entire year of 1967, which in all regards is clearly a decisive year.

The Wuhan incident

This episode from the summer of 1967 is particularly interesting, because it presents all the contradictions of a revolutionary situation at its culminating point, which of course coincides with the moment that announces its involution.

In July 1967, with the support of the conservative military, the counter-revolution of the bureaucrats dominates the enormous industrial city of Wuhan, numbering no less than 500,000 workers. The effective power is held by an army officer, Chen Zaidao. True, there are still two workers' organizations, which confront each other, causing dozens of casualties during the months of May and June. The first organization, with de facto support from the army, is called the 'One Million Heroes' and is linked to the local cadres and to the old unionists. The second, a

tiny minority, is called 'Steel', and embodies the line
of Maoism.

The central leadership, worried about the
reactionary control over the city, sends its minister
for Public Security to go on site together with a very
famous member of the 'Central Committee's Cultural
Revolution Group', named Wang Li. The latter is
extremely popular among the Red Guards, because
he is known for his outspoken 'leftist' tendencies. He
has already claimed that there was a need to purge the
army. The envoy carries a message from Zhou Enlai,
ordering the support for the 'Steel' rebel group, in
conformity with the directive addressed to the cadres
in general and to the military in particular: 'Excel in
identifying and supporting the proletarian left within
the movement.' Let us add in passing that Zhou
Enlai has taken upon himself the excruciating task
of serving as arbiter between the factions, between
the rivalling revolutionary organizations, and that,
in order to do so, he receives day and night visits
from delegates from the province. He is thus largely
responsible for the progress made by the 'great
alliance', for the unification of the 'revolutionary
committees', as well as for the discernment of what

constitutes 'the proletarian left' in these concrete situations, which are becoming more and more confused and violent.

The day of their arrival, the delegates from the Centre hold a big meeting with the rebel organizations in a city stadium. The revolutionary exaltation is reaching its high point.

We can see how all the actors from the active stage of the Revolution are well in place: the conservative cadres and their capacity for mobilization which is not to be underestimated, first in the countryside (the militias coming from the rural suburbs will participate in the repression against the Red Guards and the rebels after the turning point of 1968), but also among the workers, and of course within the administration; the rebel organizations, formed by students and workers, who count on their activism, their courage, and the support of the central Maoist group in order to gain the upper hand, even though they are often in the minority; the army, forced to choose sides; and the central power, trying hard to adjust its politics to the situation at hand.

In some cities, the situation that binds these actors together is extremely violent. In Canton, in particular, no day goes by without confrontations between the armed shock groups from rival organizations. The army decides locally to wash its hands of the affair. Hiding behind the pretext that the Decision in Sixteen Points says that one should not intervene in problems that come up during the course of the movement, the local military chief merely demands that before engaging in a street battle, one signs before him a 'declaration of revolutionary brawl'. Only the use of backup troops is prohibited. The result is that, in Canton as well, there are dozens of deaths every day throughout the summer.

In this context, the situation is about to turn sour in Wuhan. On the morning of 20 July, the shock troops of 'One Million Heroes', supported by units from the army, occupy the strategic points and launch a witch-hunt for the rebels throughout the city. An attack hits the hotel where the delegates from the central power reside. One group of military catches hold of Wang Li together with a few Red Guards and brutally beats them up. The irony of the situation: now it is the turn of the 'leftist' to be 'shown to the masses', with a sign around his neck stigmatizing him as 'revisionist', he who had seen revisionists everywhere! The minister for Public Security is locked up in his room. The university and the steel foundries, which had been the epicentre of the rebellious tendency, are taken by force by armed groups protected with tanks. However, when the news begins to spread, other units of the army take sides against the conservatives and their leader, Chen Zaidao. The 'Steel' organization mounts a counter-attack. The revolutionary committee is put under arrest. A few military manage to free Wang Li, who will leave the city by running through the woods and wastelands.

We are clearly on the verge of civil war. It will take the cold-bloodedness of the central power, as well as the firm declarations coming from numerous army units in all the provinces, to change the course of the events.

What lessons for the future can we draw from this kind of episode? In a first moment, Wang Li, his face all swollen up, is welcomed as a hero in Beijing. Jiang Qing, Mao's wife and a great rebel leader, greets him with warm accolades. On 25 July, one million people show him their support in the presence of Lin Biao. The ultra-left tendency, which believes in its good fortune, demands a radical purging of the army. This is also the moment when, in August, posters everywhere denounce Zhou Enlai as rightist.

But all this has only the appearance of an instant. True, in Wuhan, support for the rebel groups becomes mandatory, and Chen Zaidao will be replaced. But, two months later, it is Wang Li who will be brutally eliminated from the leaders' group, there will be no significant purging of the army, the importance of Zhou Enlai will only continue to grow, and the return to order will begin to make itself felt against the Red Guards and certain rebellious worker organizations.

What now becomes evident is the fundamental role of the popular army as a pillar in the Chinese party-state. The army has been given a stabilizing role in the Revolution, having been asked to support the rebel left, but there is no expectation or any tolerance for its division, which would set the scene for civil war on a large scale. Those who desire to go to such lengths will all, little by little, be eliminated. And the fact of having made a pact with these elements will cast a stubborn suspicion upon Jiang Qing herself, including, it seems, on the part of Mao.

What happens is that, at this stage of the Cultural Revolution, Mao wishes that unity should prevail

among the ranks of the rebels, particularly among the
workers, and he begins to fear the enormous damage
done by the spirit of factionalism and arrogance
among the Red Guards. In September of 1967,
after a tour in the province, he launches the slogan
'nothing essential divides the working class', which,
for those who know how to read, means first of all
that there are violent troubles between the rebellious
and conservative organizations, and, secondly, that
it is imperative to put an end to these disturbances,
to disarm the organizations, and to return the legal
monopoly of violence, as well as its political stability,
to the repressive apparatus. Starting in July, all the
while giving proof of his usual fighter's spirit and
rebelliousness (he still says, with visible delight, that
'the whole country is up in riots' and that 'to fight,
even violently, is a good thing; once the contradictions
appear in plain daylight, it is easier to solve them'),
Mao worries about the war of factions, and declares
that 'when the revolutionary committees are formed,
the petty bourgeois revolutionaries must be given the
correct leadership', he stigmatizes leftism, which 'in
fact is a form of rightism', and above all, he shows
his impatience with the fact that, since January with

the takeover of power in Shanghai 'the bourgeois and petty bourgeois ideology that was rampant among the intellectuals and the young students has ruined the situation'.

The workers enter the universities

By February 1968, after the movement's involution at the end of the summer of 1967, the conservatives think that their time for revenge has come. Mao and his group, however, are still on the alert. They launch a campaign stigmatizing the 'February counter-current' and they renew their support for the revolutionary groups and the construction of new organs of power.

In the meantime, the universities can no longer be kept under the yoke of rivalling splinter groups, given the general logic of a return to order and the perspective of an upcoming party congress charged with drawing up a balance sheet of the revolution (in fact, this congress will be held at the beginning of 1969, confirming the power of Lin Biao and the military). An example must be set, all the while avoiding the crushing pure and simple of the last Red Guards, concentrated in the buildings of the University of Beijing. The adopted solution is totally extraordinary: thousands of organized workers are called upon, without any weapons, to occupy the university, to disarm the factions and directly to ensure their authority. As the leaders' group would say later on: 'The working class must lead in every aspect', and 'the workers will stay for a long time, and even forever, in the universities'. This episode is one of the most astonishing ones of the entire period, because it renders visible the need for the violent and anarchic youth force to recognize a 'mass-based' authority higher than itself, and not only, nor even principally, the institutional authority of the recognized leaders. The moment is all the more surprising and dramatic in that certain students open fire against the workers, there will be deaths, and in the end Mao and all the leaders of the Maoist group will gather with the best-known student leaders, most notably Kuai Dafu, the venerated head of the Red Guards in the university of Beijing, and renowned nationwide. There exists a retranscription of this head-to-head meeting between the stubborn revolutionary youths and the old guard.[8] We can see

---

8   The account has been translated and amply commented upon (in Italian) by Sandro Russo, without a doubt the most

Mao expressing his profound disappointment caused by the spirit of factionalism among the youth, together with a remnant of political friendship for them, and the will to find a way out. We can clearly see that Mao, by bringing in the workers, wanted to prevent the situation from turning into one of 'military control'. He wanted to protect those who had been his initial allies and had been the bearers of enthusiasm and political innovation. But Mao is also a man of the party-state. He wants its renovation, even a violent one, but not its destruction. In the end he knows full well that by subjugating the last outpost of young rebellious 'leftists', he eliminates the last margin left to anything that is not in line (in 1968) with the recognized leadership of the Cultural Revolution: the line of party reconstruction. He knows it, but he is resigned. Because he holds no alternative hypothesis – nobody does – as to the existence of the state, and because the large majority of people, after two exalted but very trying years, want the state to exist and to make its existence known, if necessary with brute force.

---

competent and loyal analyst today of everything to do with the Cultural Revolution.

The cult of personality

We know that the cult of Mao has taken truly extraordinary forms during the Cultural Revolution. There were not only the giant statues, the *Little Red Book*, the constant invocation, in any circumstances, of the Chairman, the hymns for the 'Great Helmsman', but there was also a widespread and unprecedented one-sidedness to the references, as though Mao's writings and speeches could suffice for all occasions, even when it is a question of growing tomatoes or deciding on the use (or not) of the piano in symphonic orchestras.[9] It is striking to see that the most violent rebel groups, those who break most decisively with the bureaucratic order, are also those who push this

---

9   The examples are real, and have given rise to articles translated into French in the magazine *Pékin Informations*. There we learn how the Maoist dialectic allows one to grow tomatoes, or how to find the right line in terms of the use of the piano in symphonic music in China. Besides, these texts are extremely interesting, and even convincing, not because of their explicit content, but in terms of what it means to attempt to create *another thinking* entirely.

aspect of the situation the furthest. In particular, they are the ones who launched the formula of 'the absolute authority of Mao-Zedong Thought', and who declare the need to submit oneself to this thought even without understanding it. Such statements, we must confess, are purely and simply obscurantist.

We should add that, since all the factions and organizations that are at loggerheads with each other claim Mao's thought for their own, the expression, which is capable of designating orientations that are completely contradictory, ends up losing all meaning, except for an overly abundant use of citations whose interpretation is in a state of constant flux.

I would nonetheless like to make a few remarks in passing. On the one hand, this kind of devotion, as well as the conflict of interpretations, is totally commonplace in established religions, and among us, without being considered a pathology. Quite the contrary – the great monotheisms remain sacred cows in this regard. In comparison with the services rendered to our countries by any of the characters, whether fictive or ecclesiastical, in the recent history of these monotheisms, however, Mao has certainly been of an infinitely greater service to his people, whom he liberated simultaneously from the Japanese invasion, from the rampant colonialism of 'Western' powers, from the feudalism in the countryside and from precapitalist looting. On the other hand, the sacralization, even in terms of the biography, of great artists is also a recurring feature of our 'cultural' practice. We give importance to the dry-cleaning bills of this or that poet. If politics is, as I think, a procedure of truth, just as poetry indeed can be, then it is neither more nor less inappropriate to sacralize political creators than it is to sacralize artistic creators. Perhaps less so, all things considered, because political creation is probably rarer, certainly more risky, and it is more immediately addressed to all, and in a singular way to all those – like the Chinese peasants and workers before 1949 – whom the powers-that-be generally consider to be inexistent.

All this by no means frees us from the obligation to illuminate the peculiar phenomenon of the political cult, which is an invariant feature of communist states and parties, brought to the point of paroxysm in the Cultural Revolution.

From a general point of view, the 'cult of personality' is tied to the thesis according to which the party, as representative of the working class, is the hegemonic source of politics, the mandatory guardian of the correct line. As was said in the thirties, 'the Party is always right'. The problem is that nothing can guarantee such a representation, nor such a hyperbolic certainty as to the source of rationality. By way of a substitute for such a guarantee, it thus becomes crucial for there to be a *representation of the representation*, one that would be a singularity, legitimated precisely by its singularity alone. Finally, one person, a single body, comes to stand for this superior guarantee, in the classical aesthetic form of genius. It is also curious, by the way, to see that, trained as we are in the theory of genius in the realm of art, we should take such strong offence to it when it emerges in the order of politics. For the communist parties, between the twenties and sixties, personal genius is only the incarnation, the fixed point, of the doubtful representative capacity of the party; it is easier to believe in the rectitude and the intellectual force of a distant and solitary man than in the truth and purity of an apparatus whose local petty chiefs are well known.

In China, the question is even more complicated.

Indeed, during the Cultural Revolution, Mao incarnates not so much the party's representative capacity so much as that which discerns and struggles against the threatening 'revisionism' within the party itself. He is the one who says, or lets it be said in his name, that the bourgeoisie is politically active within the Communist Party. He is also the one who encourages the rebels, who spreads the slogan 'it is right to revolt', and encourages troubles, at the very moment when he is being canonized as the party's chairman. In this regard, there are moments when for the revolutionary masses he is less the guarantee of the really existing party than the incarnation, all by himself, of a proletarian party that is still to come. He is somewhat like a revenge of singularity upon representation.

Ultimately, we should maintain that 'Mao' is a name that is intrinsically contradictory in the field of revolutionary politics. On the one hand, it is the supreme name of the party-state, its undeniable chairman, he who, as military leader and founder of the regime, holds the historical legitimacy of the Communist Party. On the other hand, 'Mao' is the name of that which, in the party, cannot be reduced to the state's bureaucracy. This is obviously the case

in terms of the calls to revolt sent out to youth and
the workers. But it is also true within the structure
of legitimacy of the party itself. Indeed, it is often by
way of decisions that are temporarily minoritarian, or
even dissident, that Mao has ensured the continuation
of this utterly unique political experience of the
Chinese Communists between 1920 and the moment
of victory in the forties (suspicion with regard to the
Soviet counsellors, abandonment of the model of
insurrection, 'surrounding of the cities by countryside',
absolute priority to the mass line, etc.). In all aspects,
'Mao' is the name of a paradox: the rebel in power, the
dialectician put to the test by the continuing needs
of 'development', the emblem of the party-state in
search of its overcoming, the military chief preaching
disobedience to the authorities . . .[10] This is what has
given to his 'cult' a frenetic appearance, because
subjectively he accumulated the accord given to the
stately pomp of the Stalinist type, together with the
enthusiasm of the entire revolutionary youth for the old

---

10   On Mao as paradox, see the wonderful book by Henry
Bauchau, *Essai sur la vie de Mao Tsé-toung*, Flammarion,
1982.

rebel who cannot be satisfied with the existing state of affairs, and who wants to move on in the march to real communism. 'Mao' was the name for the 'construction of socialism', but also for its destruction.

In the end, the Cultural Revolution, even in its very impasse, bears witness to the impossibility truly and globally to free politics from the framework of the party-state that imprisons it. It marks an irreplaceable experience of saturation, because a violent will to find a new political path, to relaunch the revolution, and to find new forms of the workers' struggle under the formal conditions of socialism ended up in failure when confronted with the necessary maintenance, for reasons of public order and the refusal of civil war, of the general frame of the party-state.

We know today that all emancipatory politics must put an end to the model of the party, or of multiple parties, in order to affirm a politics 'without party', and yet at the same time without lapsing into the figure of anarchism, which has never been anything else than the vain critique, or the double, or the shadow, of the communist parties, just as the black flag is only the double or the shadow of the red flag.

However, our debt towards the Cultural Revolution remains enormous. Because, tied to this grandiose and courageous saturation of the motif of the party, as the contemporary of what clearly appears today as the last revolution that was still attached to the motif of classes and of the class struggle, our Maoism will have been the experience and the name of a capital transition. And without this transition, whenever there isn't anybody loyal to it, there is nothing.

A Brief Chronology of the Cultural Revolution

1. Recent prehistory (from 'One Hundred Flowers' to 'the Black Gang')

(a) Campaign 'Let a hundred flowers blossom' (1956). In June 1957, the campaign becomes a violent denunciation and persecution of 'rightist intellectuals', often qualified later on as 'evil geniuses'. The launching of the 'Great Leap Forward' in May 1958, and in August 1958 of the 'popular communes'. In August 1959, purging of Peng Dehuai (Defence Minister), who criticizes the movement of collectivization. Lin Biao replaces him.

(b) Starting in 1961, the recognition of a disastrous outcome of economic voluntarism. The Central

Committee decides to 're-adjust' the objectives. Liu Shaoqi replaces Mao Zedong as president of the Republic. Between 1962 and 1966, fifteen million copies are sold in China of Liu's works, against six million of Mao's. Publication of the historical piece by Wu Han (deputy mayor of Peking), *The Purging of Hai Rui* (an indirect criticism of this event). In September 1965, at a conference of the Politburo, Mao demands but does not obtain the condemnation of Wu Han. He retires to Shanghai.

2. The opening (from the article by Yao Wenyuan to the Decision in Sixteen Points)

(a) In collaboration with Jiang Qing, Mao's wife, Yao Wenyuan publishes a violent article in Shanghai against Wu Han. It is aimed at the mayor of Beijing, Peng Zhen, held to be the chief of the 'black gang'. In January and February 1966, a first 'Group of the Central Committee for the Cultural Revolution' is formed to judge the case, paradoxically put under the authority of Peng Zhen. This group (called 'the Group of Five') disseminates the 'February Theses', which are quite insignificant, and which tend to limit criticism.

(b) Meanwhile another group is constituted in Shanghai, under the aegis of Lin Biao and Jiang Qing, which holds a 'discussion on the literary and artistic activities in the army'. The texts are transmitted to the Military Commission of the Central Committee (organ of the highest importance). The division of the party seems consummated.

(c) In May 1966, 'enlarged' meeting of the Politburo. Nomination of a new 'Central Committee's Cultural Revolution Group', and vehement condemnation of the group of Peng Zhen in a fundamental document for all subsequent events, known as the '16 May Circular'. It is necessary, the text says, 'to criticize the representatives of the bourgeoisie infiltrated in the party, the government, the army and the cultural milieu'. By 25 May, seven students of Beida University attack the president of the university in a large-character poster. True beginning of the student mobilization.

(d) Mao leaves Beijing. The authorities send 'work groups' to the universities in order to control the movement. Between the end of May and the end of July, the so-called 'fifty days' period, in which the brutal containment by these 'work groups' is predominant.

(e) On 18 July Mao returns to Beijing. Abolition of the work groups. From 1 August until 12 August, a session of the 'enlarged' Central Committee is held. It is not according to the rules. Lin Biao uses the army to prohibit the presence of regular members and to allow the presence of revolutionaries who come from the student world. The Maoist line in these conditions obtains a brief majority. Mao publicly supports the Beida University poster. He appears before the crowd on 9 July. Political charter of the revolution: the 'Decision in Sixteen Points'. It reads in particular: 'In the great Proletarian Cultural Revolution, the only method is for the masses to liberate themselves, and any method of doing things in their stead must not be used.' That is to say, there will be no repression of the initiatives coming from the student groups.

3. The 'Red Guards' period

(a) By 20 August, arriving from high-school and university institutions, activist groups of 'Red Guards' spread out in the city, in order to 'destroy completely the old thought, culture, customs and habits'. In particular, a very harsh persecution of intellectuals and professors, once more considered, according to Mao himself, as 'evil geniuses'. Succession of immense gatherings of Red Guards in Beijing, following in particular the right given to them to circulate freely on the trains, for the sake of 'large exchanges of experience'. Criticism of Liu Shaoqi and Deng Xiaoping in posters, tracts, cartoons, small newspapers . . .

(b) Starting in November, first political incidents linked to the intervention of the Red Guards in factories. The anti-Maoists use the official unions and certain peasant militias against the revolutionaries, who themselves begin to be divided into splinter groups ('factionalism'). Violence here and there.

4. The entry of the workers and the 'power struggles'

(a) The authorities in place in Shanghai provoke disturbances by encouraging all kinds of 'economist' demands in the workers' milieux. Particularly acute problem: the salary of temporary peasant workers, and the question of bonuses. Transportation strike, and hunting down of student groups. In January 1967, a set of Red Guards and of 'rebel revolutionaries' have formed 'factory committees' by occupying the administrative offices, the means of communication, etc. They overthrow the party committee, and decide to form the 'Shanghai Commune'. Endless negotiations among the groups. Domination of the workers' groups and still a very limited presence of the old cadres of the army and state.

(b) The 'power struggles' become generalized in the entire country, starting in February 1967. Great disorder in the state and the economy. The very unequal politicization explains why the putting into place of new organs of power is anarchic and precarious. Tendency to purge and 'judge' all the old cadres, or conversely, manipulation by the cadres of 'revolutionary' groups that are more or less fake. Settling of accounts mixed in with revolutionary zeal.

(c) The central authority is then concentrated in the Central Committee's Cultural Revolution Group, the State Council, led by Zhou Enlai, and finally the Military Commission, controlled by Lin Biao. It is this authority that decides on a formula for the new powers, called the 'triple combination': one-third of representatives from the 'revolutionary masses', one-third of party cadres who have withstood the test or 'corrected' themselves, and one-third of military personnel. The revolutionary 'mass' organization must first unite among them (the 'great alliance'). The name of the new organ is 'the Revolutionary Three-in-One Combination Committee'. The first provincial committee of this kind is formed on 13 February (in the province of Kweichow).

5. Disturbances, violence and splits of all kinds

(a) At the same time that the critique of Liu Shaoqi begins in the official press (still without mentioning his name), disorder spreads everywhere. Numerous incidents of violence, including armed ones, oppose either the Maoists to the conservatives, the security and armed forces alternately to the former and to the latter, or else, finally, the Maoist groups among themselves. The mass organizations split up very frequently. The revolutionary leadership also divides itself. One tendency aims to unify the revolutionary organizations as quickly as possible, and everywhere to put into place committees that will give due space to the old cadres. In fact, this tendency quickly seeks to reconstruct the party. Zhou Enlai, who, it is true, is in charge of the maintenance of the elementary functions of the state, is the most active figure in this direction. Another tendency wants to eliminate a very large number of cadres, and to expand the purge to the administration, including the army. Its best-known representatives are Wang Li and Qi Benyu.

(b) In July, the Wuhan incident puts the region and, finally, the whole country, in a climate of civil war. The army in this city openly protects the traditional cadres and the workers' organizations that are tied to them. Wang Li, sent on an envoy by the central authority, which seeks to support the 'rebels', is locked up and beaten. It is necessary for external military forces to intervene. The unity of the army is thus threatened.

(c) Appearance of the posters against Zhou Enlai. During all of August, moments of anarchic violence, particularly in Canton. Weapon depots are sacked. Dozens of people die every day. The British Embassy is set on fire in Beijing.

6. The beginning of the return to order and the end of the revolution properly speaking

(a) In September 1967, Mao, after a tour in the province, decides in favour of the 'reconstructive' line. Fundamentally, he supports Zhou Enlai and gives the army an extended role (where the factions do not manage to reach an agreement, there will be 'military control'). The extreme-left group (Wang Li) is eliminated from the central organs of power. 'Study sessions of Mao Zedong Thought' are organized for everyone, often under the aegis of the military. Slogans: 'Support the left, and not the factions', based on a statement included in Mao's report: 'Nothing essential divides the working class.'

(b) In many places, this rectification is practised by way of a violent repression of the Red Guards, and even of the rebel workers, and as an occasion for political revenge (this is the 'February Counter-Current'). As a result, Mao calls once again for action by the end of March 1968: it is necessary to defend the revolutionary committees and to fear neither disturbances nor factionalism.

(c) However, this is the last 'mass' brawl. The central authority decides to put an end to the last bastions of the student revolt, which are abandoned to the often bloody wars among splinter groups, all the while avoiding, at least in Beijing, direct military control. Detachments of workers are sent into the universities. The central group of the Cultural Revolution receives the most famous 'leftist' students, who have physically resisted the entry of these workers. It turns out to be a dialogue of the deaf (the most notorious 'rebel' student, Kuai Dafu, will be arrested).

(d) The directive 'the working class must be in command in everything' seals the end of the Red Guards and of the revolutionary rebels, and in the name of 'struggle, criticism, reform', opens a phase devoted to the reconstruction of the party. A huge number of young revolutionaries is sent to the countryside, or to faraway camps.

7. Marking the aftermath

(a) The Ninth Congress of the Party, in April 1969, ratifies an authoritarian return to order, largely structured by the army (45 per cent of the members of the Central Committee) under the direction of Lin Biao.

(b) This militarist period, which is terribly oppressive, leads to new violent confrontations in the midst of the party. Lin Biao is eliminated (probably assassinated) in 1971.

(c) Until Mao's death, a long and complex period, marked by the endless conflict between Deng Xiaoping and many old cadres who have returned to business under the protection of Zhou Enlai, on one hand, and, on the other, the 'Gang of Four', which embodies the memory of the Cultural Revolution (Yao Wenyuan, Zhang Chunqiao, Jiang King and Wang Hongwen).

(d) Right after the death of Mao, in 1976, the four are arrested. Deng takes over power for a long period, which is indeed largely defined by the implantation of capitalist methods (during the Cultural Revolution, he was called 'the second highest among the officials who, despite being of the party, have taken the capitalist road'), with the maintenance of the party-state.

III

The Paris Commune:
A Political Declaration on Politics[1]

The political parties, groups, unions and factions that have claimed to be representative of the workers and the people long maintained a formal fidelity to the Paris Commune. They adhered to Marx's concluding statement in his admirable text *The*

Civil War in France: 'Working men's Paris, with its Commune, will be forever celebrated as the glorious harbinger of a new society.'

They regularly visited the Mur des fédérés, the monument evoking the twenty thousand shot dead in May 1871. Marx again: 'Its martyrs are enshrined in the great heart of the working class.'

Does the working class have a heart? Today, in any case, little is remembered, and badly so. The Paris Commune was recently removed from [French] history syllabuses, in which, however, it had barely

---

a multiple of multiples, so that everything that is must be seen as a pure multiple, in *Logiques des mondes* he makes the cohesion of appearing, or the 'there' of a world, depend on what he calls its transcendental, that is, the structure of order that measures the identities and differences in this world by assigning varying degrees of greater or lesser intensity to the existence of its objects. The following chapter studies the possibility of real change within a given regime of appearing, with specific references to a well-known sequence in revolutionary politics, namely, the Paris Commune of 1871. The result is a complete rearticulation of the conditions in which a given space can become the site of a radically transformative event. *Translator's note*.

occupied a place. The public ranks are swollen with the direct descendants of the *Versaillais*, those for whom communism is a criminal utopia, the worker an outdated Marxist invention, the revolution a bloody orgy, and the idea of a non-parliamentary politics a despotic sacrilege.

As usual, however, the problem is not one of memory but of truth. How are we to concentrate the political truth of the Commune today? Without neglecting textual and factual supports, what is at stake here is to reconstitute, by means that will be largely philosophical, this episode of our history in its irreducibility.

Of course, when I say 'our' history, it has to do with the 'we' of a politics of emancipation, the 'we' whose virtual flag remains red, and not the tri-coloured one flown by the killers of the spring of 1871.

Reference points, 1 – the facts

I shall begin with a selection of dated examples. This will form the first part, after which I shall reorder the account according to new categories (situation, appearing [*apparaître*],[2] site, singularities, event, inexistent aspect [*inexistent*] . . .).

In the very middle of the nineteenth century, in France, Napoleon III is in power. He typifies the racketeering and authoritarian balance-sheet of the Republican Revolution of February 1848. This kind of outcome had been practically guaranteed only a few months after the insurrection that brought down Louis-Philippe in June 1848, when the republican petty bourgeoisie consented to, and even supported, the massacring of Parisian workers by Cavaignac's troops. Just as, in 1919, the German social-democratic petty bourgeoisie were to set up the distant possibility of a Nazi hypothesis by organizing the massacre of the Rosa Luxemburg-led Spartacists.

On 19 July 1870, the French government, too self-confident and victim to Bismarck's devious manoeuvres,

---

2   The French verb *apparaître* (to appear) is usually better translated as a noun (appearing, appearance). The phrase 'dans l'apparaître' I have most often rendered as 'in the domain of appearing'.

declares war on Prussia. On 2 September, the disaster at
Sedan occurs and the Emperor is captured.[3] This danger
leads to a partial arming of the Parisian population in
the form of a National Guard, the internal framework
of which is constituted by workers. But the internal
situation is in fact determinant: on 4 September, after
large demonstrations, the Hôtel-de-Ville is stormed
and the empire overthrown. But as was the case in
1830 and 1848, power is at once monopolized behind
the scenes by a group of 'Republican' politicians,
i.e., the Jules Favres, Simon and Ferry ('the Republic
of the Juleses' as Henri Guillemin will say), Emile
Picard and Adolphe Thiers, all of whom wish for
only one thing: to negotiate with Bismarck in a bid
to contain the working-class political insurgency.
But they must put people off the scent, so in order
to subdue the resolve of the Parisian population they
immediately proclaim a Republic, although they fail
to specify any constitutional content; and in order to

---

3   The battle of Sedan, September 1870, ended when
Napoleon III capitulated to the Prussians, who then proceeded
to march on Paris. *Translator's note*.

circumvent patriotic sentiment they call themselves
'the Government of National Defence'. Under these
conditions the masses leave them to get on with it, and
instead join in the resistance, which the long siege on
Paris by the Prussians will exacerbate.

In October, in shameful conditions, Bazaine
surrenders at Metz with the bulk of the French
army. Then, all sorts of little government schemes,
recounted in minute detail in the great books Henri
Guillemin dedicated to the 1870 war and the origins
of the Commune, lead to the surrender of Paris
and the armistice of 28 January 1871. A majority
of Parisians have long been in no doubt that this
government is in reality a government of 'National
Defection'.

But it is also a government of bourgeois defence
against popular movements. Its problem is now to find
a way to disarm the Parisian workers of the National
Guard. There were at least three reasons why the
politicians in power were able to think the situation
to their advantage. First, they had managed with great
haste to get an Assembly elected that was dominated by
rural and provincial reaction, indeed, a sort of *chambre*

introuvable of the extreme right that was *legitimist*[4]
and socially vengeful. Against revolution nothing beats
an election: it is this same maxim that De Gaulle,
Pompidou and their allies on the official left will revive
in June 1968. Second, the principal and foremost
recognized revolutionary leader, Blanqui, is in prison.
Third, the clauses of the armistice leave Paris encircled
by Prussian troops from the North and the East.

Early on the morning of 18 March, some military
detachments try to seize the cannons held by the
National Guard. The attempt comes up against an
impressive, spontaneous mobilization in the workers'
quartiers by the Parisian people, and notably by the
Parisian women. The troops withdraw; the government
flees to Versailles.

On 19 March, the Central Committee of the National
Guard, being the worker leadership that had been
elected by the units of the Guard, makes a political
declaration. This is a fundamental document to which
I will return in detail.

---

4   The French adjective 'legitimist' derives from the
Legitimists, who were French adherents to the 'legitimate'
Bourbon dynasty overthrown in 1830. *Translator's note.*

On 26 March, the new Parisian authorities organize the election of a Commune of 90 members.

On 3 April, the Commune attempts a first military sortie to confront the troops that the government, with Prussian authorization, has redirected against Paris. The sortie fails. Those taken prisoner by the troops, including two highly respected members of the Commune, Flourens and Duval, are massacred. A sense of the ferocity of the repression to come fills the air.

On 9 April, the Commune's best military leader, the Polish republican Dombrowski, has some success, notably in recapturing Asníres.

On 16 April, supplementary elections for the Commune are held in an absolutely above-board manner and in the greatest calm.

Between 9 May and 14 May, the military situation worsens considerably in the south-west *suburbs*. The forts of Issy and Vanves fall.

All this while (between the end of March and the middle of May), the people of Paris pursue their lives inventively and peacefully. All kinds of social measures concerning work, education, women and the arts are debated and decided upon. For an idea of the prioritization of issues, note, for example, that on 18 May – the government army will enter Paris *en masse* on 21 May – a vote is held on the number of classes to create in primary schools.

In fact Paris is at once peaceful and extraordinarily politicized. Purely descriptive accounts by witnesses to the scene are rare: the non-militant intellectuals generally support Versailles, and most of them (Flaubert, Goncourt, Dumas fils, Leconte de Lisle, Georges Sand . . .) make base remarks. None of the intellectuals are more admirable than Rimbaud and Verlaine, declared partisans of the Commune, and Hugo, who, without understanding anything, will instinctively and nobly oppose the repression.

One chronicle is absolutely extraordinary. Its attribution to Villiers de l'Isle Adam is regularly contested and then reaffirmed. In any case, it makes intensely visible the combination of peace and political vivacity that the Commune had installed in the streets of Paris:

One enters, one leaves, one circulates, one gathers. The laughter of Parisian children interrupts political discussions. Approach the groups, listen. A whole people entertain profound matters. For the first time workers can be heard exchanging their appreciations on things that hitherto only philosophers had tackled. There is no trace of supervisors; no police agents obstruct the street hindering passers-by. The security is perfect.

Previously, when this same people went out intoxicated for its *bals de barríre*,[5] the bourgeoisie distanced itself, saying quietly: 'If these people were free, what would become of us? What would become of them? They are free and dance no longer. They are free and they work. They are free and they fight.'

When a man of good faith passes close by them today, he understands that a new century has just hatched and even the most sceptical remains wondrous.

---

5   A tradition of dance-halls created under Louis XIV, *bals de barríre* were located on the outskirts of town and frequented by the lower classes. *Translator's note*.

Between 21 May and 28 May, the troops of Versailles take Paris barricade by barricade, the final combats taking place in the workers' redoubts of the north-east *arrondissements*: the 11th, the 19th, the 20th . . . The massacres succeed each other without interruption, continuing well after the 'bloody week'. At least twenty thousand people are shot dead. Fifty thousand are arrested.

Thus commences the Third Republic, which is still held by some today to be the golden age of 'citizenship'.

Reference points, 2 – the classical interpretation

At this very time, Marx proposed an account of the Commune that is wholly inscribed in the question of the state. For him, it comprises the first historical case in which the proletariat assumes its transitory function of the direction, or administration, of the entire society. From the Commune's initiatives and impasses he is led to the conclusion that the state machine must not be 'taken' or 'occupied', but broken.

Let's note in passing that the chief fault of the analysis probably lies in the notion that between March and May 1871 it was the question of power that was the order of the day. Whence those tenacious 'critiques' that have become commonplaces: what the Commune supposedly lacked was decision-making capacity. *If* it had immediately marched on Versailles, *if* it had seized the gold of the Bank of France . . . To my mind, these 'ifs' lack real content. In truth, the Commune had neither the means to address them properly, nor in all likelihood the means to arrive at them.

Marx's account in fact is ambiguous. On the one hand, he praises everything that appears to lead to a dissolution of the state and, more specifically, of the nation-state. In this vein he notes: the Commune's abolition of a professional army in favour of directly arming the people; all the measures it took concerning the election and revocability of civil servants; the end it put to the separation of powers in favour of a decisive and executive function; and its internationalism (the financial delegate of the Commune was German, the military leaders Polish, etc.). But, on the other hand, he deplores incapacities that are actually statist incapacities [*incapacités étatiques*]: its weak military centralization; its inability to define financial priorities; and, its shortcomings concerning the national question, its address to other cities, what it did and did not say about the war with Prussia, and its rallying of provincial masses.

It is striking to see that, twenty years later, in his 1891 preface to a new edition of Marx's text, Engels formalizes the Commune's contradictions in the same way. He shows, in effect, that the two dominant political forces of the 1871 movement, the Proudhonians and the Blanquists, ended up doing exactly the opposite of their manifest ideology. The Blanquists were partisans of centralization to excess and of armed plots in which a small number of resolute men would take power, to exercise it authoritatively to the advantage of the working masses. But instead they were led to proclaim a free federation of communes and the destruction of state bureaucracy. Proudhonians were hostile to any collective appropriation of the means of production and promoted small, self-managed enterprises. Yet they ended up supporting the formation of vast worker associations for the purpose of directing large-scale industry. Engels quite logically concludes from this that the Commune's weakness lay in the fact that its ideological forms were inappropriate for making decisions of state. And, moreover, that the result of this opposition is quite simply the end of Blanquism and of Proudhonism, making way for a single 'Marxism'.

But how would the current that Marx and Engels represented in 1871, and even much later, have been more adequate to the situation? With what extra means would its presumed hegemony have endowed the situation?

The fact of the matter is that the ambiguity of Marx's account will be carried [*sera levée*] both by the social-democratic disposition and by its Leninist radicalization, that is, in the fundamental motif of the party, for over a century.

In effect, the 'social-democratic' party, the party of the 'working class' – or the 'proletarian' party – and then later still the 'communist' party, is simultaneously free in relation to the state and in a position to exercise power.

It is a purely political organ that is constituted by subjective support – by ideological rupture – and as such is exterior to the state. With respect to domination, it is free; it bears the thematic of revolution or of the destruction of the bourgeois state.

But the party is also the organizer of a centralized, disciplined capacity that is entirely bent on taking state power. It bears the thematic of a new state, the state of the dictatorship of the proletariat.

It can be said, then, that the party *realizes* the ambiguity of the Marxist account of the Commune, gives it body. It becomes the political site of a fundamental tension between the non-state, even anti-state, character of a politics of emancipation, and the statist character of the victory and duration of that politics. Moreover, this is the case irrespective of whether the victory is insurrectional or electoral: the mental schema is the same.

This is why the party will engender (particularly from Stalin onwards) the figure of the party-state. The party-state is endowed with capacities designed to resolve problems the Commune left unresolved: a centralization of the police and of military defence; the complete destruction of bourgeois economic decisions; the rallying and submission of the peasants to workers' hegemony; the creation of a powerful international, etc.

It is not for nothing that, as legend has it, Lenin danced in the snow the day Bolshevik power reached and surpassed the 72 days in which the Paris Commune's entire destiny was brought to a close.

Yet, although it may have provided a solution to the statist problems that the Commune was unable to resolve, it remains to be asked whether in solving them the party-state did not suppress a number of *political* problems that, to its merit, the Commune had been able to discern.

What is in any case striking is that, retroactively thought through the party-state, the Commune is reducible to two parameters: first, to its *social* determination (workers); and second, to a heroic but defective exercise of *power*.

As a result the Commune gets emptied of all properly political content. It is certainly commemorated, celebrated and claimed, but only as a pure point for the articulation of the social nature of state power. But if that is all it consists in, then the Commune is *politically obsolete*. For it is rendered so by – what Sylvain Lazarus has proposed to call – the Stalinist political mode, for which the unique place of politics is the party.

That is why its *commemoration* also happens to proscribe its *reactivation*.

On this point there is an interesting story concerning Brecht. After the war, Brecht returns prudently to 'socialist' Germany, in which Soviet troops lay down the law. He sets out in the year of 1948 by stopping in Switzerland to get news of the situation from abroad. During his stay he writes, with the aid of Ruth Berlau, his lover at the time, a historical play called *The Days of the Commune*. This is a solidly documented work in which historical figures are combined with popular heroes. It is a play that is more lyrical and comical than epic; it is a good play, in my view, although rarely performed. Now, upon arriving in Germany, Brecht suggests staging *The Days of the Commune* to the authorities. Well, in the year 1949, the authorities in question declare such a performance inopportune! As socialism is in the process of being victoriously established in East Germany, there could be no reason to return to a difficult and outmoded episode of proletarian consciousness such as the Commune. Brecht, in sum, had not chosen the good calling-card. He had not understood that, since Stalin had defined Leninism – reduced to the cult of the party – as 'the Marxism of the epoch of victorious revolutions', returning to defeated revolutions was pointless.

That said, what is Brecht's interpretation of the Commune? In order to judge it, let's read the last three stanzas of the song in the play titled *Resolution of the Communards*:

Realizing that we won't persuade you
Into paying us a living wage
We resolve that we will take the factories from
    you
Realizing that your loss will be our gain

Realizing that we can't depend on
All the promises our rulers make
We've resolved for us the Good Life starts with
    freedom
Our future must be built by our dictate

Realizing that the roar of cannon
Are the only words that speak to you
We prove to you that we have learned our lesson
In future we will turn the guns on you[6]

---

6   Bertolt Brecht, *The Days of the Commune*, trans. by Clive Barker and Arno Reinfrank, Eyre Methuen, 1978.

Clearly, the general framework here remains that of the classical interpretation. The Commune is cast as a combination of the social and of power, of material satisfaction and of cannons.

Reference points, 3 – a Chinese reactivation

During the Cultural Revolution, and especially between 1966 and 1972, the Paris Commune is reactivated and very often mentioned by Chinese Maoists, as if, caught in the grip of the rigid hierarchy of the party-state, they sought new references outside of the Revolution of 17 October and official Leninism. Thus, in the Sixteen-Point Decision of August 1966, which is a text probably mostly written by Mao himself, a recommendation is given to seek inspiration in the Paris Commune, particularly as concerns the electing and recalling of the leaders of the new organizations emerging from the mass movements. After the overthrow of the municipality of Shanghai by revolutionary workers and students in January 1967, the new organ of power takes 'the Shanghai Commune' as its name, pointing to the fact that some of the Maoists were trying to link up politically to questions of power and state in a mode other than that which had been canonized by the Stalinist form of the party.

Yet, these attempts are precarious. This can be witnessed in the fact that, as power had been 'seized' and it was imperative to install the new organs of that provincial and municipal power, the name 'Commune' is quickly abandoned, and replaced by the much more indistinct title of 'Revolutionary Committee'. This can also be witnessed in the centennial commemoration of the Commune in China in 1971. That this commemoration involved more than just commemorating, that it still contained the elements of a reactivation, is evident in the magnitude of the demonstrations. Millions of people march all throughout China. But little by little the revolutionary parenthesis is closed, which is evident in the official text published for the occasion, a text that some of us read at the time, and that a far fewer number of us have conserved and can reread (which has probably become very difficult for someone Chinese to do . . .). The text in question is: *Long Live the Victory of the Dictatorship of the Proletariat! In Commemoration of the Centenary of the Paris Commune.*[7]

It is totally ambivalent.

Significantly, it contains in the epigraph a formula written by Marx at the time of the Commune itself:

> If the Commune should be destroyed, the struggle would only be postponed. The principles of the Commune are eternal and indestructible; they will present themselves again and again until the working class is liberated.

This choice confirms that even in 1971 the Chinese consider that the Commune is not simply a glorious (but obsolete) episode of the history of worker insurrections but a historical exposition of principles that are to be reactivated. Hear, also, a statement echoing Marx's statement, possibly one of Mao's: 'If the Cultural Revolution fails, its principles will remain no

---

7   *Long Live the Victory of the Dictatorship of the Proletariat! In Commemoration of the Centenary of the Paris Commune*, Foreign Language Press, 1971.

less the order of the day.' Which indicates once more
that the Cultural Revolution extends a thread that is
linked more to the Commune than to October 1917.

The Commune's relevance is likewise made evident
by the content of its celebration, in which Chinese
communists are opposed to Soviet leaders. For
example:

> At the time when the proletariat and the
> revolutionary people of the world are marking
> the grand centenary of the Paris Commune, the
> Soviet revisionist renegade clique is putting
> on an act, talking glibly about 'loyalty to the
> principles of the Commune' and making itself up
> as the successor to the Paris Commune. It has
> no sense of shame at all. What right have the
> Soviet revisionist renegades to talk about the
> Paris Commune?

It is within the framework of this ideological
opposition between creative revolutionary Marxism
and retrograde statism that the text situates both Mao's
contribution and, singularly, the Cultural Revolution
itself, in continuity with the Commune:

The salvoes of the Great Proletarian Cultural Revolution initiated and led by Chairman Mao himself have destroyed the bourgeois headquarters headed by that renegade, hidden traitor and scab Liu Shao-chi and exploded the imperialists' and modern revisionists' fond dream of restoring capitalism in China.

Chairman Mao has comprehensively summed up the positive and negative aspects of the historical experience of the dictatorship of the proletariat, inherited, defended and developed the Marxist–Leninist theory of the proletarian revolution and the dictatorship of the proletariat and solved, in theory and practice, the most important question of our time – the question of consolidating the dictatorship of the proletariat and preventing the restoration of capitalism.

The capital formula is 'consolidating the dictatorship of the proletariat'. To invoke the Paris Commune here is to understand that the dictatorship of the proletariat cannot be a simple statist formula, and that pursuing the march toward communism necessitates recourse to a revolutionary mobilization of the masses. In other words, just as the Parisian workers of 18 March 1871 had done for the first time in history, it was considered necessary to invent within an ongoing revolutionary experience – always a somewhat precarious and unpredictable decision – new forms for a proletarian state. What is more, early on in the piece the Maoists had already declared the Cultural Revolution to be 'the finally discovered form of the dictatorship of the proletariat'.

Nevertheless, the general conception articulating politics and state remains unchanged. The attempted revolutionary reactivation of the Paris Commune remains inscribed in the anterior account and, in particular, is still dominated by the tutelary figure of the party. This is clearly shown in the passage on the Commune's shortcomings:

The fundamental cause of the failure of the Paris Commune was that, owing to the historical conditions, Marxism had not yet achieved a dominant position in the workers' movement and a proletarian revolutionary Party with Marxism as its guiding thought had not yet come into being. [. . .] Historical

experience shows that where a very favourable
revolutionary situation and revolutionary
enthusiasm on the part of the masses exist,
it is still necessary to have a strong core
of leadership of the proletariat, that is, 'a
revolutionary party . . . built on the Marxist–
Leninist revolutionary theory and in the
Marxist–Leninist revolutionary style.'

Although the final citation about the Party is by Mao,
it could have just as easily been by Stalin. This is why,
in spite of its activism and its militancy, the Maoist
vision of the Commune ultimately remained prisoner
of the party-state framework and, hence, of what I
have called the 'first account'.

At the end of this sketch of the classical
interpretation, and of that which is in exception to it,
we can say, then, that today the political *visibility* of
the Paris Commune is not at all evident. At least, that
is, if what we mean by 'today' is the moment when
we have to take up the challenge of thinking politics
outside of its subjection to the state and outside of the
framework of parties or of the party.

And yet the Commune was a political sequence that,

precisely, did not situate itself in such a subjection or
in such a framework.

The method will thus consist in putting to one side
the classical interpretation and tackling the political
facts and determinations of the Commune using a
completely different method.

Preliminaries: what is the 'left'?

To start with, let's note that before the Commune
there had been a number of more or less armed
popular and workers' movements in France in a
dialectic with the question of state power. We can
pass over the terrible days of June 1848 when the
question of power is thought not to have been posed:
the workers, cornered and chased from Paris upon
the closing of national workshops, fought silently,
without leadership, without perspective. Despair,
fury, massacres. But there were the *Trois Glorieuses*
of July 1830 and the fall of Charles V; there was
February 1848 and the fall of Louis-Philippe; and,
lastly, there was 4 September 1870 and the fall of
Napoleon III. In the space of forty years, young
Republicans and armed workers brought about the

downfall of two monarchies and an empire. That is exactly why, considering France to be the 'classic land of class struggle', Marx wrote those masterpieces *The Class Struggles in France*, *The 18ᵗʰ Brumaire of Louis Bonaparte* and *The Civil War in France*.

As regards 1830, 1848 and 1870, we must note that they share a fundamental trait, one that is all the more fundamental as it is still of relevance today. The mass political movement is largely proletarian. But there is general acceptance that the final result of the movement will involve the coming to power of cliques of Republican or Orleanist politicians. The gap between politics and state is tangible here: the parliamentary projection of the political movement attests in effect to a political incapacity *as to the state*. But it is also noticeable that this *incapacity is in the medium term experienced [vécu] as a failing of the movement itself and not as the price of a structural gap between the state and political invention*. At bottom, the thesis prevails, subjectively, within the proletarian movement, that there is or ought to be a continuity between a political mass movement and its statist bottom line. Hence the recurrent theme of 'betrayal' (i.e. the politicians in power betray

the political movement. But did they ever have any
other intention, indeed, any other *function*?). And
each time this hopeless motif of betrayal leads to
a liquidation of political movement, often for long
periods.

That is of utmost interest. Recall that the final
result of the popular movement (*'Ensemble!'*) of
December 1995[8] and of the *sans-papiers* movement
of Saint-Bernard[9] was the election of Jospin, against
whom the – empirically justified – cries of 'betrayal'
were not long in coming. On a larger scale, May 1968
and its 'leftist' sequence wore themselves out rallying
to Mitterrand's aid already well before 1981. Further
away still, the radical novelty and political expectancy

---

8   'Tous Ensemble!' was a directive of the 1995 winter
strikes in France that brought two million workers and
their supporters to the streets. They were sparked, among
other things, by plans by the Juppé government to attack
the national health system and introduce a shaky pension
scheme. *Translator's note.*
9   The *sans-papiers* (undocumented workers) movement
is associated with the Saint-Bernard church, which was
occupied by hundreds of African workers in 1996 protesting
the persecutory effects of French government laws.
Translator's note.

of the Resistance movements between 1940 and 1945
came to little after the Liberation when the old parties
were returned to power under the cover of De Gaulle.

Jospin, Mitterrand and their kind are the Jules
Favres, the Jules Simons, the Jules Ferries, the Thiers
and the Picards of our conjuncture. And, today, we
are still being called upon to 'rebuild the left'. What a
farce!

It is true that the memory of the Commune also
testifies to the constant tactics of adjustment that
parliamentary swindlers undertake in relation to
eruptions of mass politics: the *Mur des fédérés*,
meagre symbol of martyred workers, does it not lie
on the side of the grand avenue Gambetta, that shock
parliamentarian and founder of the Third Republic?[10]

But to all this the Commune stands as an exception.

For *the Commune is what, for the first and to this
day only time, broke with the parliamentary destiny
of popular and workers' political movements*. On the

---

10   Léon Michel Gambetta (1838–82) was a French states-
man and prime minister (1881–82). A parliamentary
opponent of Napoleon III, he was Minister of the Interior in
the Government of National Defence, and helped form the
Third Republic. *Translator's note.*

evening of the resistance in the workers' districts, 18 March 1871, when the troops had withdrawn not having been able to take the cannons, there could have been an appeal to return to order, to negotiate with the government, and to have a new clique of opportunists pulled out of history's hat. This time there would be nothing of the sort.

Everything is concentrated in the declaration by the Central Committee of the National Guard, which was widely distributed on 19 March:

> The proletarians of Paris, amidst the failures and treasons of the ruling classes, have understood that the hour has struck for them to save the situation by taking into their own hands the direction of public affairs.

This time, this unique time, destiny was not put back in the hands of competent politicians. This time, this unique time, betrayal is invoked as a state of things to avoid and not as the simple result of an unfortunate choice. This time, this unique time, the proposal is to deal with the situation solely on the basis of the resources of the proletarian movement.

Herein lies a real *political declaration*. The task is to think its content.

But first a structural definition is essential: *Let's call 'the left' the set of parliamentary political personnel that proclaim that they are the only ones equipped to bear the general consequences of a singular political movement.* Or, in more contemporary terms, that they are the only ones able to provide 'social movements' with a 'political perspective'.

Thus we can describe the declaration of 19 March 1871 precisely as *a declaration to break with the left.*

That is obviously what the Communards had to pay for with their own blood. Because, since at least 1830, 'the left' has been the established order's sole recourse during movements of great magnitude. Again in May 1968, as Pompidou very quickly understood, only the PCF was able to re-establish order in the factories. The Commune is the unique example of a break with the left on such a scale. This, in passing, is what sheds light on the exceptional virtue, on the paradigmatic contribution – far greater than 17 October – it had for Chinese revolutionaries between 1965 and 1968, and for French Maoists between 1966 and 1976: periods when the task was precisely to break with all subjection to that fundamental emblem, the 'left', an emblem that – whether they were in power or in opposition (but, in a profound way, a 'great' Communist party is *always* in power) – the Communist parties had turned into.

True, after being crushed, leftist 'memory' absorbed the Commune. The mediation of that paradoxical incorporation took the form of a parliamentary combat for amnesty for exiled or still-imprisoned Communards. Through this combat the left hoped for a risk-free consolidation of its electoral power. After that came the epoch – about which I've said a word – of commemorations.

Today, the Commune's political visibility must be restored by a process of dis-incorporation: born of rupture with the left, it must be extracted from the leftist hermeneutics that have overwhelmed it for so long.

In doing this, let's take advantage of the fact that the left, whose baseness is constitutive, has now fallen so low that it no longer even makes a pretence of remembering the Commune.

But the operation is not easy. It requires that you grant me the patience to put in place some operators and a new *découpage* of events.

The Commune is a site – ontology of the Commune

Take any situation whatsoever. *A multiple that is an object of this situation – whose elements are indexed by the transcendental of this situation – is a site if it happens to count itself within the referential field of its own indexation.* Or again: a site is a multiple that happens to behave in the situation with regard to itself as with regard to its elements, in such a way as to support the being of its own appearing.

Even if the idea is still obscure, we can begin to see its content: a site is a singularity because it evokes its being in the appearing of its own multiple composition. It makes itself, in the world, the being-there of its being. Among other consequences, this means that the site gives itself an intensity of existence. A site is a being that happens to exist by itself.

The whole point will be to argue that 18 March 1871 is a site.

So, at the risk of repeating myself, I shall go over once more, with a view to a singular construction, all the terms of the situation 'Paris at the end of the Franco-Prussian War of 1870'. We are in the month of

March 1871. After a semblance of resistance, and shot through with fear of revolutionary and worker Paris, the interim government of bourgeois 'Republicans' capitulates to Bismarck's Prussians. In order to consolidate this political 'victory' – very comparable to Pétain's reactionary revenge in 1940 (where preferring an arrangement with the external enemy to exposure to the internal enemy) – it has an assembly with a royalist majority hastily elected by a frightened rural world, an assembly that sits in Bordeaux.

Led by Thiers, the government hopes to take advantage of the circumstances to annihilate the political capacity of the workers. But on the Parisian front, the proletariat is armed in the form of a National Guard, owing to its having been mobilized during the siege on Paris. In theory, the Parisian proletariat has many hundreds of cannons at its disposal. The 'military' organ of the Parisians is the Central Committee, at which assemble the delegates of the various battalions of the National Guard, battalions that are in turn linked to the great working-class *quartiers* of Paris – Montmartre, Belleville and so forth.

Thus we have a divided world whose logical organization – what in philosophical jargon could be called its transcendental organization – reconciles intensities of political existence according to two sets of antagonistic criteria. Concerning the representative, electoral and legal dispositions, one cannot but observe the pre-eminence of the Assembly of traditionalist Rurals,[11] Thiers's *capitulard* government, and the officers of the regular army, who, having been licked without much of a fight by Prussian soldiers, dream of doing battle with the Parisian workers. That is where the power is, especially as it is the only power recognized by the occupier. On the side of resistance, political intervention, and French revolutionary history, there is the fecund disorder of Parisian worker organizations, which intermingles with the Central Committee of the twenty *quartiers*, the Federation of the Trade Unions, a few members of the International, and local military committees. In truth, the historical consistency of this world, which

---

11   The Assembly of 'Rurals' was the nickname of the National Assembly of 1871, so called because it comprised mainly reactionary monarchists – provincial landlords, officials, rentiers and traders – elected in rural districts. The were about 430 monarchists among the Assembly's 630 deputies. *Translator's note.*

had been separated and disbanded [*déli*] owing to the war, is held together only by the majority conviction that no kind of worker capacity for government exists. For the vast majority of people, including often the workers themselves, the politicized workers of Paris are simply incomprehensible. These workers are the non-existent aspect [*l'inexistant propre*] of the term 'political capacity' in the uncertain world of the spring of 1871. But for the bourgeoisie they are still too existent, at least physically. The government receives threats from the stock exchange saying: 'You will never have financial operations if you do not get rid of these reprobates.' First up, then, an imperative task, and a seemingly easy one to carry out: disarm the workers and, in particular, retrieve the cannons distributed throughout working-class Paris by the military committees of the National Guard. It is this initiative that will make of the term '18 March' (a single day – such as it is exposed in the situation 'Paris in spring 1871') a site, that is, that which *presents itself* in the appearing of a situation.

More precisely, 18 March is the first day of the event calling itself the Paris Commune, that is, the exercise of power by Socialist or Republican political militants and organizations of armed workers in Paris from 18 March to 28 May 1871. The balance-sheet of this sequence is the massacring of many tens of thousands of 'rebels' by the troops of the Thiers government and the reactionary Assembly.

What is, exactly, in terms of its manifest content, this beginning called 18 March? Our answer is: the appearing of a worker-being – to this very day a social symptom, the brute force of uprisings, and a theoretical threat – in the space of governmental and political capacity.

And what happens? Thiers orders General Aurelles de Paladine to retrieve the cannons held by the National Guard. Close to three in the morning a coup is carried out by some select detachments. A complete success, so it seems. On the walls an announcement by Thiers and his ministers can be read; it bears the paradoxes of a split transcendental evaluation: 'Let the good citizens separate from the bad; let them aid the public force.' Nevertheless, by eleven in the morning the coup has totally failed. The soldiers have been encircled by hundreds of ordinary women, backed up by anonymous workers and members of the National Guard acting on their own behalf. Many of the soldiers fraternize. The cannons are taken back. General Aurelles de Paladine panics, seeing in it the great red peril: 'The Government calls upon you to defend your homes, your families, your property. Some misguided men, obeying only some secret leaders, turn the cannons kept back from the Prussians against Paris.' According to him, it is a matter of 'putting an end to the insurrectional Committee, whose members represent only Communist doctrines, and who would pillage Paris and bury France'. All to no avail.

Despite being without veritable leadership, the rebellion extends, occupying the whole city. The armed workers' organizations make use of the barracks, public buildings, and finally the Hôtel-de-Ville, which, under a red flag, will be the site and symbol of the new power. Thiers saves himself, escaping via a hidden staircase. The minister Jules Favre jumps out of a window. The whole governmental apparatus disappears and sets itself up at Versailles. Paris is delivered to the insurrection.

The eighteenth of March is a site because, apart from whatever else appears here under the ambiguous transcendental of the world 'Paris in spring 1871', it appears as the striking, and totally unforeseeable, beginning of a rupture (true, still without concept) with the very thing that had established the norm of its appearing. Note that '18 March' is the title of a chapter from the militant Lissagaray's magnificent *History of the Paris Commune of 1871*, published in 1876. This chapter is concerned, naturally, with the 'women of 18 March', the 'people of 18 March', attesting to the fact that '18 March', now a predicate, has come to be included as an essential element in evaluating the possible outcomes of the day's turn of events. Lissagaray sees clearly that, under the sign of an eruption of being, the fortuities of 18 March have brought about an immanent overturning of the laws of appearing. Indeed, from the fact that the working people of Paris, overcoming the dispersion of their political framework, prevented a governmental act carried out with precision and rapid force (the seizure of the cannons), results the obligation that an unknown capacity appear, an unprecedented power by which '18 March' comes to appear, under the injunction of being, as an element of the situation that it is.

In fact, from the point of view of well-ordered

appearing, the possibility of a popular and worker governmental power purely and simply does not exist. This is the case even for the militant workers themselves, who use the vocabulary of the 'Republic' indistinctly. On the evening of 18 March, the members of the Central Committee of the National Guard – the only effective authority of the city whose legal tutors have absconded – remain more or less convinced they should not be sitting at the Hôtel-de-Ville, reiterating that they 'do not have a mandate for government'. In accordance with our conception of 'the left', this amounts to saying that they baulk at breaking with it. It is only with the sword of circumstances hanging over their heads that they end up deciding, as Édouard Moreau – a perfect nobody – will dictate to them the morning of 19 March to 'proceed to elections, to provide for the public services, and to protect the town from a surprise'. With this act *nolens volens*, they directly constitute themselves, against any allegiance to the parliamentary left, as a political authority. In so doing, they invoke '18 March' as the beginning of that authority, an authority as a consequence of 18 March.

Hence it is essential to understand that 18 March is a site because it imposes itself on all the elements that help to bring about its existence as that which, on the basis of the indistinct content of worker-being, 'forcibly' calls for a wholly new transcendental evaluation of the latter's intensity. The site '18 March', this empirical '18 March' in which is dealt out the impossible possibility of worker existence, is, thought as such, a subversion of the rules of political appearing (of the logic of power) by means of its own active support.

The Commune is a singularity – logic of the Commune, 1

As to the thought of its pure being, a site is simply a multiple that happens to be an element of itself. We have just illustrated this by the example of 18 March, a complicated set of peripeteia whose result is that '18 March' gets instituted, in the object '18 March', as the exigency of a new political appearing, as forcing an unheard-of transcendental evaluation of the political scene.

Yet a site must be thought not simply in terms of

the ontological particularity that I have just identified, but also according to the logical unfolding of its consequences.

Indeed, the site is a figure of the instant. It appears only to then disappear. Veritable duration, that is, the time a site opens or founds, pertains only to its consequences. The enthusiasm of 18 March 1871 is most certainly the founding of the first worker power in history, but when on 10 May the Central Committee proclaims that to save the 'revolution of 18 March, which it had begun so well', it would 'put an end to controversies, put down the malignants, quell rivalry, ignorance, and incapacity', its boastful desperation betrays everything that had appeared, by means of the distribution and enveloping of political intensities, in the city for the past two months.

That said, what is a consequence? This point is crucial for theorizing the historical appearing of a politics. I'll obviously have to skip over the technical details of that theorization for now. The simplest thing to do is to fix a value for the relation of consequence between two terms in a situation by the mediation of their degree of existence. If an element a of a situation is such that the existence of a has a value of p, and if

the element b of the same situation exists to the degree
of q, we can postulate that b will be a consequence
of a in equal measure to the dependency of these
intensities, or, if you like, their order. If, for example,
on the scale measuring the intensities of existence
proper to a certain situation, q is greatly inferior to p,
we can validate the dependency of b to a.

We can say, then, that a consequence is a strong
or weak relation between existences. The degree to
which one thing is the consequence of another is never
independent of the intensity of existence they have in
the situation under consideration. The aforementioned
declaration of the Central Committee of 10 May 1871,
then, may be read as a thesis on the consequences. It
registers:

— The very strong intensity of existence on the
day of 18 March 1871, the day of that revolution
that had 'begun so well'.
— The implicitly disastrous degree of existence
of political discipline in the worker camp two
months later ('bad will', 'rivalry', 'ignorance',
'incapacity').
— A desire (though unfortunately abstract) to

bring the value of the consequences of the politics
in course level with the power of existence of its
disappeared origin.

A site is the appearing/disappearing of a multiple
whose paradox is self-belonging. The logic of a site
involves the distribution of intensities, around the
vanishing point, in which the site consists. So, then,
we shall begin at the beginning: what is the value
of existence of the site itself? After which we can
proceed to consider what can be deduced as regards
its consequences.

The value of the site's existence cannot be prescribed
from anything in its ontology. A sudden appearance
can be no more than a barely 'perceptible' local
apparition (it is pure image since there is no perception
here). And further: its disappearing cannot leave any
trace. Indeed, it may well be that ontologically taking
on the marks of 'true' change (self-belonging and
disappearance in the instant), a site is nevertheless,
owing to its existential insignificance, hardly different
from a simple continuation of the situation.

For example, on Tuesday 23 May 1871, when nearly
the whole of Paris is at the hands of the Versaillais

soldiery – who shoot workers by the thousands on staircases all over the city – and the Communards, who fight barricade by barricade, no longer have any military or political leadership, the remainder of the Central Committee make their last proclamation, which is hastily stuck up on a few walls and, as Lissagaray said with sombre irony, is a 'proclamation of victors'. The proclamation calls for the conjoint dissolution of the (legal) Assembly of Versailles and the Commune, the retreat of the Parisian army, a provisional government entrusted to the delegates of big cities, and a reciprocal amnesty. How to qualify this sad 'Manifesto'? Owing to its sheer incongruity, it cannot be reduced to the normality of the situation. This Manifesto still expresses, be it in a derisory way, the Commune's self-certitude, its just conviction of having marked the beginning of a new politics. This document is something that, although the wind of the barracks will carry it *aux oubliettes*, can be legitimately held to be one of the site's elements. But in the savage dawn of the worker insurrection, its value of existence is very weak. What is in question here is the site's singular power. This Central Committee manifesto can of course be ontologically situated in that which holds the evental syntagm the 'Paris Commune' together, but as a sign of decomposition or of powerlessness it leads the singularity of this syntagm back to the margins of a pure and simple modification of the situation, or to its simple mechanical development, and is lacking in veritable creation.

On this point, let's cite the terrible passage dedicated to the Commune's last moments by Julien Gracq in *Lettrines*. I included this extract in the preface to my *Théorie du sujet* in 1981 as an indication that all of my philosophical efforts aimed to contribute, however slightly, to preventing us (as the inheritors of the Cultural Revolution and May 1968) from becoming '*dealers in herring vouchers*'.

Gracq had been rereading the third volume of the autobiography of Communard leader Jules Vallès titled *L'insurgé*. Here is a fragment of his commentary:

Marx was indulgent of the leadership of the Commune, whose shortcomings he had perfectly seen. The revolution also had its Trochu and its Gamelin. Vallès's frankness consternates, and might cause one to take horror at that proclamatory leadership, those chand'vins revolutionaries, on whom the barricaders of Belleville spat as they passed by during the last days of the blood-soaked week. There is no excuse to lead the good fight when one leads it so lightly.

A kind of atrocious nausea arises while following the *Ubuesque* masquerade, the pathetic disorder, of the last pages, wherein the unfortunate Commune delegate – no longer daring to show his sash which he clasped under his arms in a newspaper – a sort of incompetent district official, of petroleur Charlot leaping between shell blasts, incapable of doing anything at all, treated harshly by the rebels who bare their teeth, wanders like a lost dog from one barricade to another distributing in disorderly fashion vouchers for herrings, bullets, and fire, and imploring the spiteful crowd – which was hard on his heels because of the fix into which he had plunged it – pitifully, lamentably, 'Leave me alone, I ask you. I need to think alone.'

In his exile as a courageous incompetent, he must have sometimes awoken at night, still hearing the voices of all the same series of people

who were to be massacred in a few minutes, and
who cried so furiously at him from the barricade:
'Where are the orders? Where is the plan?'[12]

So that this kind of disaster doesn't arise, the
appearing of the site must have a force of appearing
that compensates for its evanescence. Nothing has
potential for an event [*est en puissance d'événement*]
but a site whose value of existence is maximal. This
was the case in all certainty on 18 March 1871, when,
women at the front, the working people of Paris forbade
the army from disarming the National Guard. But it is
no longer the case concerning the Commune's political
leadership as of the end of April.

We will call a site whose intensity of existence is
not maximal a *fact*.

We will call a site whose intensity of existence is
maximal a *singularity*.

You will notice that the repressive force of
the Versaillais is accompanied by a propaganda

12   cf. Julian Gracq, *Lettrines: Œuvres complètes*. Gallimard,
1989, pp. 205–206; and Alain Badiou, *Théorie du sujet*,
Seuil, 1982, pp. 14–15.

that systematically desingularizes the Commune, presenting it as a monstrous set of facts to be (forcibly) returned to the normal order of things. This results in some extraordinary statements, such as the one published in the conservative journal *Le Sícle* on 21 May 1871, right in the middle of the massacre of workers: 'The social difficulties have been resolved or are in the process of being resolved.' It could not have been better put. On the other hand, as early as 21 March, only three days after the insurrection, Jules Favre was given to proclaiming that Paris was at the mercy of 'a handful of villains, holding above the rights of the Assembly I don't know what kind of rapacious and bloody ideal'. In the appearing of a situation, strategic and tactical choices oscillate between fact and singularity, because it is, as always, a question of relating to a logical order of circumstances.

When a world finally comes to be situated – from what becomes of the site in it – and is placed between singularity and fact, then it is down to the network of consequences that it comes to decide.

18 March and its consequences –
logic of the Commune, 2

A singularity diverges further from simple continuity than a fact because it is attached to an intensity of maximal existence. If, now, we are further compelled to make a distinction between weak and strong singularities, it is so that we can establish the consequences woven by an evanescent site with the elements of the situation that presented it in the world.

To be brief, we shall say that *existing* maximally for the time of its appearing/disappearing accords a site the power [*puissance*] of a singularity. And further, that to *make (something) exist* maximally is all the force such a singularity has.

We shall reserve the name of event for a strong singularity.

A few remarks are in order about the predicative distinction strength/weakness as it applies to singularities (that is, to sites whose transcendental intensity of existence is maximal).

Now, it can be seen that in work of the nature of the appearing of truth, the Paris Commune, crushed in blood in two months, is nonetheless much more significant than 4 September 1870, the date when the political regime of the Second Empire collapsed and the Third Republic – which lasted seventy years – began. This in no way relates to the actors: on 4 September it was also the working people who, under a red flag, invaded the square of the Hôtel-de-Ville and, as Lissagaray recounted so vividly, caused the officials to go to pieces: 'Important dignitaries, fat functionaries, ferocious Mamelukes, imperious ministers, solemn chamberlains, moustached generals, shake pitifully on 4 September, like a bunch of weak hams.' On one hand, then, we have an insurrection that establishes nothing of duration; on the other, a day that changes the state. But 4 September was to be confiscated by bourgeois politicians primarily concerned to re-establish the order of property, while the Commune, Lenin's ideal referent, will inspire a century of revolutionary thought, thus meriting the famous evaluation Marx gave of it before its bloody end:

The Commune was . . . the initiation of the Social Revolution of the 19th century. Whatever therefore its fate at Paris, it will make *le tour du monde*. It was at once acclaimed by the working class of Europe and the United States as the magic word of delivery.[13]

Let's posit then that 4 September is a weak singularity, because it is aligned on the general development of European states, which converge on the parliamentary form. Moreover, let's say that the Commune is a strong singularity because it proposes to thought a rule of emancipation, and is relayed – perhaps against the grain – by October 1917 and, more specifically, by the summer of 1967 in China, and May 1968 in France. For is it not only the exceptional intensity of its sudden appearing that counts (i.e. the fact that they have to do with violent and creative episodes within the domain of appearance) but what, over time, such evanescent emergences set up by way of uncertain and glorious consequences.

Beginnings can, then, be measured by the re-beginnings they authorize.

---

13   Karl Marx, *Civil War in France*, First Draft, Archives of Marx and Engels, 1934, p. 173. Available online at www. marx2mac.com/M&E/CWFdrf71.html#s0

It is in that aspect of a singularity which continues by means of the concentration, external to it, of its intensity that we can judge whether an aleatory adjunction to the world warrants being considered – beyond facts and continuities – not just as a singularity but as an event.

The Commune is an event –
logic of the Commune, 3

Everything, then, depends on the consequences. And note that there exists no stronger a transcendental consequence than that of making something appear in a world which had not existed in it previously. This was the case on 18 March 1871, when a collection of unknown workers were thrust to the centre of the political scene, workers unknown even to specialists of the revolution – those old surviving 'quarante-huitards' – whose inefficient logomachy unfortunately did much to encumber the Commune. Let's return to 19 March, and to the first declarations made by the Central Committee, the only accountable organ to emerge from the 18 March insurrection: 'Let Paris and France put together the bases of an acclaimed Republic with all its consequences, the only government that will close forever the era of invasion and civil wars.' By whom is this unprecedented political decision signed? Twenty people, three-quarters of whom are proletarians that the circumstances alone constitute and identify. Right on cue with the well-worn theme of 'foreign agents', the governmental *Officiel* complacently asks: 'Who are the members of the Committee? Are they communists, Bonapartists, or Prussians?' Instead, they were yesterday's inexistent workers, brought into a provisionally maximal political existence as the consequence of an event.

Hence, we can identify a strong singularity by the fact that, for a given situation, it has the consequence of making an inexistent term exist in it.

In more abstract fashion, we will posit the following definition: *given a site (a multiple affected with self-belonging) which is a singularity (its intensity of existence, as instantaneous and as 'evanescent' as it may be, is nevertheless maximal), we will say that this site is a strong singularity, or an event, if, in consequence of the (maximal) intensity of the site, something whose value of existence was nil in the situation takes on a positive value of existence.*

So, what I'm basically saying is that an event *has, as a maximally true consequence of its (maximal) intensity of existence, the existence of an inexistent*.

This obviously implies a violent paradox. Because if an implication is maximally true and so also is its antecedent, then its consequent must be; we thus come to the seemingly untenable conclusion whereby, under the effect of an event, the inexistent aspect of a site comes to exist absolutely.

And indeed: the unknown members of the Central Committee, who were politically inexistent in the world the day before, come to exist absolutely the same day as their appearing. The Parisian people obey their proclamations, encourage them to occupy the public buildings, and turn out for the elections they organize.

The paradox can be analysed under three headings. In the first place, the principle of this overturning of worldly appearing from inexistence to absolute existence is a vanishing principle. All the event's power is consumed in the existential transfiguration. As evental multiplicity, 18 March 1871 has not the least stability.

Secondly, if the inexistent aspect of a site must

ultimately capture, in the order of appearing, a maximal intensity, it is only to the extent that this intensity henceforth take the place of what has disappeared; its maximality is the subsisting mark, in the world, of the event itself. The 'eternal' existence of an inexistent consists in the trace [*tracé*] or statement, in the world, of the evanescent event. The proclamations of the Commune, the first worker power in universal history, comprise a historic existent whose absoluteness manifests the coming to pass in the world of a wholly new ordering of its appearing, a mutation of its logic. The existence of an inexistent aspect is that by which, in the domain of appearing, the subversion of worldly appearing by subjacent being is played out. It is the logical marking of a paradox of being, an ontological chimera.

Destruction – logic of the Commune, 4

Lastly, an inexistent aspect must come again within the space in which existence is henceforth held together. Worldly order cannot be subverted to the point of being able to require the abolition of a logical law

of situations. Every situation has at least one proper
inexistent aspect, and if this aspect happens to be
sublimated into absolute existence, another element
of the site must cease to exist, thereby keeping the
law intact and ultimately preserving the coherence of
appearing.

In 1896, adding another conclusion to his *History
of the Commune of 1871*, Lissagaray makes two
observations. The first is that the band of reactionaries
and workers' assassins of 1871 is still in place.
Parliamentarism playing its part, it has even been
augmented with 'some bourgeois fiefs who, under the
mask of democrats, facilitate its advances'. The second
is that the people henceforth constitutes its own force:
'Three times [in 1792, in 1848 and in 1870] the French
proletariat made the Republic for others; now it is
ripe for its own.' In other words, the Commune event,
begun on 18 March 1871, did not have the effect of
destroying the dominant group and its politicians. But
something more important was destroyed: the political
subordination of workers and the people. What was
destroyed was of the order of subjective incapacity:
'Oh!' exclaims Lissagaray, 'they are not uncertain
of their capacities, these workers of the country and

the towns.'[14] The absolutization of worker political existence (the existence of the inexistent), convulsive and crushed, had all the same destroyed the necessity of a basic form of subjection; that is, the subjection of a possible proletarian politics to the scheming of (leftist) bourgeois politicians. Like every veritable event, the Commune had not *realized* a possible, it had created one. This possible is simply that of an independent proletarian politics.

That a century later the necessity of subjection to the left has been reconstituted, or rather reinvented under the very name of 'democracy', is another story, another sequence in the often tormented history of truths. It remains the case that where an inexistent aspect (worker political capacity) was held in place, the destruction of what legitimated this inexistence (subjective incapacity) came to pass. At the beginning of the twentieth century, what occupies the place of death is no longer

---

14   Proper-Olivier Lissagaray, 'The Eighteenth of March', *History of the Commune of 1871*, trans. Eleanor Marx Aveling, International Publishing, 1898, pp. 78–87. Trans. of 'Le 18 mars', *Histoire de la commune de 1871*, La Découverte, 2000, pp. 111–119.

worker political awareness [*conscience*], but – even if it was not yet realized – the prejudice that classes are natural in character, and that it is the millenary vocation of proprietors and the wealthy to conserve social and state power. The Paris Commune accomplished this destruction for the future, even in the apparent putting to death of its own super-existence [*surexistence*].

Here we have a transcendental maxim: if, in the form of an evental consequence, what was worth nothing comes to equal the whole, then an established given within the domain of appearing is destroyed. What had sustained the cohesion of a world is struck with non-existence; such that, if the transcendental indexation of beings is the (logical) base of the world, then it is with good reason that it must be said: 'the world shall rise on new foundations'.

When the world is violently enchanted by the absolute consequences of a paradox of being, the whole of the domain of appearing, threatened with the local destruction of a customary evaluation, must come again to constitute a different distribution of what exists and what does not.

Under the eruption being exerts on its own

appearing, nothing in a world can come to pass except the possibility – mingling existence and destruction – of another world.

Conclusion

I believe this other world resides for us in the Commune, yet altogether elsewhere than in its subsequent existence, what I have called its *first* existence, that is, in the party-state and its social worker referent. Instead, it exists in the observation that a political rupture is always a combination of a subjective capacity and an organization – totally independent of state – of the consequences of that capacity.

Further, it is important to argue that such a rupture is always a rupture with the left, in the formal sense I have given to that term. Today, this amounts to saying a rupture with the representative form of politics, or, if one wants to go further in the way of founded provocation, a rupture with 'democracy'.

The notion that the consequences of a political capacity are obligatorily of the order of power and state administration belongs to the first account of the Commune, not to the one that interests us. Instead, our problem is rather to return – prior to this first account (prior to Lenin, if you will) – to what was alive but defeated in the Commune: to the fact that a politics appears when a *declaration* is at one and the same time a *decision as to the consequences*, and, thus, when a decision is active in the form of a previously unknown collective discipline. Because we must never stop recalling that those who are nothing can only stick to a wager on the consequences of their appearing in the element of a new discipline, a discipline that is a practical discipline of thought. The Party in Lenin's sense certainly comprised the creation of such a discipline, but one that was ultimately subordinated to constraints of State. Today's task, being undertaken notably by the Organisation Politique, is to support the creation of such a discipline subtracted from the grip of the state, the creation of a thoroughly political discipline.

IV

The Idea of Communism

My aim today is to describe a conceptual operation to which, for reasons that I hope will be convincing, I will give the name 'the Idea of communism'. No doubt the trickiest part of this construction is the most general one, the one that involves explaining what an Idea is, not just with respect to political truths (in which case the Idea is that of communism) but with respect to any truth (in which case the Idea is a modern version of what Plato attempted to convey to us under the names of *eidos*, or *idea*, or even more precisely the Idea of the Good). I will leave a good deal of this generality implicit,[1] in

---

1 The theme of the Idea appears gradually in my work. It was no doubt already present in the late '80s from the moment when, in *Manifesto for Philosophy*, I designated my undertaking as a 'Platonism of the multiple', which would require a renewed investigation into the nature of the Idea. In *Logics of Worlds*, this investigation was expressed

order to be as clear as possible regarding the Idea of communism.

Three basic elements – a political, a historical and a subjective one – are needed for the operation of 'the Idea of communism'.

First, the political element. This concerns what I call a truth, a political truth. Regarding my analysis of the Chinese Cultural Revolution (a political truth if ever there was one), one reviewer for a British newspaper remarked – merely from noting my positive account of this episode of Chinese history (which *he* of

---

as an imperative: 'true life' was conceived of as life lived in accordance with the Idea, as opposed to the maxim of contemporary democratic materialism, which commands us to live without any Idea. I examined the logic of the Idea in greater detail in *Second Manifesto for Philosophy*, in which the notion of ideation, and thus of the operative, or working, value of the Idea is introduced. This was backed up by a multifaceted commitment to something like a renaissance of the use of Plato. For example: my seminar, which for the past two years has been entitled 'For today: Plato!'; my film project, *The Life of Plato*; and my complete translation (which I call a 'hypertranslation') of *The Republic*, renamed *Du Commun(isme)* and redivided into nine chapters, which I hope to complete and publish in 2010.

course regards as a sinister, bloody catastrophe) – that it was 'not hard to feel a certain pride in workaday Anglo-Saxon empiricism, which inoculates us [the readers of the *Observer*] against the tyranny of pure political abstraction'.[2] He was basically taking pride in the fact that the dominant imperative in the world today is 'Live without an Idea'. So, to please him, I will begin by saying that a political truth can, after all, be described in a purely empirical way: it is a concrete, time-specific sequence in which a new thought and a new practice of collective emancipation arise, exist, and eventually disappear.[3] Some examples of this can

2   Rafael Behr, 'A denunciation of the "Rat Man"', *Observer*, 1 March 2009. *Translator's note*.
3   The rarity of politics, in the guise of sequences destined for an immanent end, is very powerfully argued by Sylvain Lazarus in his book *L'Anthropologie du Nom* (Seuil, 1996). He calls these sequences 'historical modes of politics', which are defined by a certain type of relationship between a politics and its thought. My philosophical elaboration of a truth procedure would appear to be very different from this (the concepts of event and genericity are completely absent from Lazarus's thought). I explained in *Logics of Worlds* why my philosophical enterprise is nevertheless compatible with Lazarus's, which puts forward a thought of politics elaborated

even be given: the French Revolution, from 1792 to 1794; the People's War of Liberation in China, from 1927 to 1949; Bolshevism in Russia, from 1902 to 1917; and – unfortunately for the *Observer*'s critic, although he probably won't like my other examples all that much either – the Great Cultural Revolution, at any rate from 1965 to 1968. That said, formally, that is, philosophically, I am speaking about a truth procedure here, in the sense that I have been giving this term since *Being and Event*. I'll come back to this shortly. But let's note right away that every truth procedure prescribes a Subject of this truth, a Subject who – even empirically – cannot be reduced to an individual.

Now for the historical element. As the time frame of political sequences clearly shows, a truth procedure is inscribed in the general becoming of Humanity, in a local form whose supports are spatial, temporal and anthropological. Designations such as 'French' or 'Chinese' are the empirical indices of this localization.

---

from the standpoint of politics itself. Note that for him, too, obviously, the question of the time frame of the modes is very important.

They make it clear why Sylvain Lazarus speaks of 'historical modes of politics', not simply of 'modes'. There is in fact a historical dimension of a truth, although the latter is in the final analysis universal (in the sense that I give this term in my *Ethics* book, for example, or in my *Saint Paul: The Foundation of Universalism*) or eternal (as I prefer to put it in *Logics of Worlds* or in my *Second Manifesto for Philosophy*). In particular, we will see that, within a given type of truth (political, but also amorous, artistic or scientific), the historical inscription encompasses an interplay between types of truth that are different from one another and are therefore situated at different points in human time in general. In particular, there are retroactive effects of one truth on other truths that were created before it. All this requires a transtemporal availability of truths.

And finally, the subjective element. What is at issue is the possibility for an individual, defined as a mere human animal, and clearly distinct from any Subject, to decide[4] to become part of a political truth

4   This aspect of decision, of choice, of the Will, in which the Idea involves an individual commitment, is increasingly

procedure. To become, in a nutshell, a militant of this truth. In *Logics of Worlds*, and in a simpler manner in the *Second Manifesto for Philosophy*, I describe this decision as an incorporation: the individual body and all that it entails in terms of thought, affects, potentialities at work in it, and so forth, becomes one of the elements of another body, the body-of-truth, the material existence of a truth in the making in a given world. This is the moment when an individual declares that he or she can go beyond the bounds (of selfishness, competition, finitude . . .) set by individualism (or animality – they're one and the same thing). He or she can do so to the extent that, while remaining the individual that he or she is, he or she can also become, through incorporation, an active part of a new Subject. I call this decision, this will, a subjectivation.[5] More

---

present in the works of Peter Hallward. It is telling that, as a result, references to the French and Haitian Revolutions, in which these categories are the most visible, should now haunt all his work.

5 In my *Théorie du Sujet*, published in 1982, the couple formed by subjectivation and the subjective process plays a fundamental role. This is an additional sign of my tendency, as Bruno Bosteels contends in his work (including his English

generally speaking, a subjectivation is always the process whereby an individual determines the place of a truth with respect to his or her own vital existence and to the world in which this existence is lived out.

I call an 'Idea' an abstract totalization of the three basic elements: a truth procedure, a belonging to history, and an individual subjectivation. A formal definition of the Idea can immediately be given: an Idea is the subjectivation of an interplay between the singularity of a truth procedure and a representation of History.

In the case that concerns us here, we will say that an Idea is the possibility for an individual to understand that his or her participation in a singular political process (his or her entry into a body-of-truth) is also, in a certain way, a *historical* decision. Thanks to the Idea, the individual, as an element of the new Subject, realizes his or her belonging to the movement of History. For about two centuries (from Babeuf's 'community of equals' to the 1980s), the word

---

translation of the book, recently published with a remarkable commentary on it), to return little by little to some of the dialectical intuitions of that book.

'communism' was the most important name of an Idea located in the field of emancipatory, or revolutionary, politics. To be a communist was of course to be a militant of a Communist Party in a given country. But to be a militant of a Communist Party was also to be one of millions of agents of a historical orientation of all of Humanity. In the context of the Idea of communism, subjectivation constituted the link between the local belonging to a political procedure and the huge symbolic domain of Humanity's forward march towards its collective emancipation. To give out a leaflet in a marketplace was also to mount the stage of History.

So it is clear why the word 'communism' cannot be a purely political name: for the individual whose subjectivation it supports, it effectively connects the political procedure to something other than itself. Nor can it be a purely historical term. This is because, lacking the actual political procedure, which, as we shall see, contains an irreducible element of contingency, History is but empty symbolism. And finally, it cannot be a purely subjective, or ideological, word either. For subjectivation operates 'between' politics and history, between singularity and the projection of this singularity into a symbolic whole and, without such materialities and symbolizations, it cannot attain the status of a decision. The word 'communism' has the status of an Idea, meaning that, once an incorporation has taken place, hence from within a political subjectivation, this term denotes a synthesis of politics, history and ideology. That is why it is better understood as an operation than as a concept. The communist Idea exists only at the border between the individual and the political procedure, as that element of subjectivation that is based on a historical projection of politics. The communist Idea is what constitutes the becoming-political Subject of the individual as also and at the same time his or her projection into History.

If only so as to move towards the philosophical turf of my friend Slavoj Žižek,[6] I think it might help to

---

6   Slavoj Žižek is probably the only thinker today who can simultaneously hew as closely as possible to Lacan's contributions and argue steadfastly and vigorously for the return of the Idea of communism. This is because his real master is Hegel, of whom he offers an interpretation that is completely novel, inasmuch as he has given up subordinating it to the theme of Totality. There are two ways of rescuing

clarify things by formalizing the operation of the Idea in general, and of the communist Idea in particular, in the register of Lacan's three orders of the Subject: the real, the imaginary and the symbolic. First, we will posit that the truth procedure itself is the real on which the Idea is based. Next, we will allow that History exists only symbolically. In effect, it cannot appear. In order to appear, belonging to a world is necessary. However, History, as the alleged totality of human becoming, has no world that can locate it in an actual existence. It is a narrative constructed after the fact. Finally, we will grant that subjectivation, which projects the real into the symbolic of a History, can only be imaginary, for one major reason: no real can be symbolized as such. The real exists, in a given world, and under very specific conditions that I will come back to later. However, as Lacan said over and over, it is

---

the Idea of communism in philosophy today: either by abandoning Hegel, not without regret, incidentally, and only after repeated considerations of his writings (which is what I do), or by putting forward a different Hegel, an unknown Hegel, and that is what Žižek does, based on Lacan (who was a magnificent Hegelian – or so Žižek would claim – at first explicitly and later secretly, all along the way).

unsymbolizable. So the real of a truth procedure cannot be 'really' projected into the narrative symbolism of History. It can be so only imaginarily, which doesn't mean – far from it – that this is useless, negative, or ineffective. On the contrary, it is in the operation of the Idea that the individual finds the capacity to consist 'as a Subject'.[7] We will therefore assert the following: the Idea exposes a truth in a fictional structure. In the specific case of the communist Idea, which is operative when the truth it deals with is an emancipatory political sequence, we will claim that 'communism' exposes this sequence (and consequently its militants) in the symbolic order of History. In other words, the communist Idea is the imaginary operation whereby an individual subjectivation projects a fragment of the political real into the symbolic narrative of a History.

---

7   To live 'as a Subject' can be taken in two ways. The first is like 'to live as an Immortal', a maxim translated from Aristotle. 'As' means 'as if one were'. The second way is topological: incorporation in effect means that the individual lives 'in' the subject-body of a truth. These nuances are clarified by the theory of the body-of-truth on which *Logics of Worlds* concludes, a decisive conclusion but, I must admit, one that is still too condensed and abrupt.

It is in this sense that one may appropriately say that the Idea is (as might be expected!) ideological.[8]

It is essential today to understand that 'communist' can no longer be the adjective qualifying a politics. An entire century of experiences both epic in scope and appalling was required to understand that certain phrases produced by this short-circuiting between the real and the Idea were misconceived, phrases such as 'Communist Party' or 'Communist State' – an oxymoron that the phrase 'Socialist State' attempted to get around. The long-term effects of the Hegelian origins of Marxism are evident in this short-circuiting. For Hegel in fact, the historical exposure of politics was not an imaginary subjectivation, it was the real as such. This was because the crucial axiom of the dialectic as he conceived of it was: 'The True is the process of its own becoming' or – what amounts to the same – 'Time is the being-there of the concept'. As a result, in line with the Hegelian philosophical

---

8   Basically, if you really want to understand the tired-out word 'ideology', the simplest thing to do is to stay as close as possible to its derivation: something can be said to be 'ideological' when it has to do with an Idea.

heritage, we are justified in thinking that, under the name of 'communism', the historical inscription of revolutionary political sequences or of the disparate fragments of collective emancipation reveals their truth: to move forward according to the meaning of History. This latent subordination of truths to their historical meaning entails that we can speak 'in truth' of communist politics, communist parties and communist militants. It is clear, however, that we need to avoid any such 'adjectification' today. To combat such a thing, I have many times had to insist that History does not exist, which is in keeping with my conception of truths, namely, that they have no meaning, and especially not the meaning of History. But I need to clarify this verdict today. Of course, there is no real of History and it is therefore true, transcendentally true, that it cannot exist. Discontinuity between worlds is the law of appearance, hence of existence. What *does* exist, however, under the real condition of organized political action, is the communist Idea, an operation tied to intellectual subjectivation and that integrates the real, the symbolic and the ideological at the level of the individual. We must bring this Idea back, by uncoupling it from any predicative usage. We must rescue the Idea, but also free the real from any immediate fusion with it. Only political sequences that it would ultimately be absurd to label as communist can be recovered by the communist Idea as the potential force of the becoming-Subject of individuals.

So we must begin with truths, with the political real, in order to define the Idea in terms of the threefold nature of its operation: politics-real, history-symbolic and ideology-imaginary.

Let me begin by reminding you of a few of my usual concepts, in a very abstract, simple form.

I call an 'event' a rupture in the normal order of bodies and languages as it exists for any particular situation (if you refer to *Being and Event* [1988] or *Manifesto for Philosophy* [1989]) or as it appears in any particular world (if you refer instead to *Logics of Worlds* [2006] or the *Second Manifesto for Philosophy* [2009]). What is important to note here is that an event is not the realization of a possibility that resides within the situation or that is dependent on the transcendental laws of the world. An event is the creation of new possibilities. It is located not merely at the level of objective possibilities but at the level of the possibility of possibilities. Another way of putting this is: with respect to a situation or a world, an event paves the way for the possibility of what – from the limited perspective of the make-up of this situation or the legality of this world – is strictly impossible. If we keep in mind here that, for Lacan, the real = the impossible, the intrinsically real aspect of the event will be readily seen. We might also say that an event is the occurrence of the real as its own future possibility.

I call a 'State' or 'state of the situation' the system of constraints that limit the possibility of possibilities. By the same token, we will say that the State is that which prescribes what, in a given situation, is the impossibility specific to that situation, from the perspective of the formal prescription of what is possible. The State is always the finitude of possibility, and the event is its infinitization. For example, what is the State comprised of today with regard to its political possibilities? Well, the capitalist economy, the constitutional form of government, the laws (in the juridical sense) concerning property and inheritance, the army, the police . . . Through all these systems, all these apparatuses, including, of course, those that Althusser called 'ideological State apparatuses', which could be defined by their one common goal – preventing the communist Idea from designating a possibility – we can see how the State organizes and maintains, often by force, the distinction between what is possible and what isn't. It follows clearly from this that an event is something that can occur only to the extent that it is subtracted from the power of the State.

I call a 'truth procedure' or a 'truth' an ongoing organization, in a given situation (or world), of the consequences of an event. It will be noted at once that a fundamental randomness, that of its evental origins, partakes in every truth. I call 'facts' the consequences of the existence of the State. It will be observed that intrinsic necessity is always on the side of the State. So it is clear that a truth cannot be made up of pure facts. The non-factual element in a truth is a function of its orientation, and this will be termed subjective. We will also say that the material 'body' of a truth, in so far as it is subjectively oriented, is an exceptional body. Making unabashed use of a religious metaphor, I will say that the body-of-truth, as concerns what cannot be reduced to facts within it, can be called a glorious body. With respect to this body, which is that of a new collective Subject in politics, of an organization composed of individual multiples, we will say that it shares in the creation of a political truth. In the case of the State of the world in which this creation is at work, we will speak of historical facts. History as such, made up of historical facts, is in no way subtracted from the power of the State. History is neither subjective nor glorious. History should instead be said to be the history of the State.[9]

So we can now return to our subject, the communist Idea. If, for an individual, an Idea is the subjective operation whereby a specific real truth is imaginarily projected into the symbolic movement of a History, we can say that an Idea presents the truth as if it were a fact.

---

9 That history is the history of the State is a thesis introduced into the field of political speculation by Sylvain Lazarus, but he has not yet published all its consequences. Here, too, one could say that my ontologico-philosophical concept of the State, as it was introduced in the mid-'80s, is distinguished by a different (mathematical) point of departure and a different (metapolitical) destination. However, its compatibility with Lazarus's is confirmed in one major regard: no political truth procedure can be confused, in its very essence, with the historical actions of a State.

In other words, the Idea presents certain facts as symbols of the real of truth. This was how the Idea of communism allowed revolutionary politics and its parties to be inscribed in the representation of a meaning of History the inevitable outcome of which was communism. Or how it became possible to speak of a 'homeland of socialism', which amounted to symbolizing the creation of a possibility – which is fragile by definition – through the magnitude of a power. The Idea, which is an operative mediation between the real and the symbolic, always presents the individual with something that is located between the event and the fact. That is why the endless debates about the real status of the communist Idea are irresolvable. Is it a question of a regulative Idea, in Kant's sense of the term, having no real efficacy but able to set reasonable goals for our understanding? Or is it an agenda that must be carried out over time through a new post-revolutionary State's action on the world? Is it a utopia, if not a plainly dangerous, and even criminal, one? Or is it the name of Reason in History? This type of debate can never be concluded for the simple reason that the subjective operation of the Idea is not simple but complex. It involves real sequences of emancipatory politics as its essential real condition, but it also presupposes marshalling a whole range of historical facts suitable for symbolization. It does not claim (as this would amount to subjecting the truth procedure to the laws of the State) that the event and its organized political consequences are reducible to facts. But neither does it claim that the facts are unsuitable for any historical trans-scription (to make a Lacanian sort of play on words) of the distinctive characters of a truth. The Idea is a historical anchoring of everything elusive, slippery and evanescent in the becoming of a truth. But it can only be so if it admits as its own real this aleatory, elusive, slippery, evanescent dimension. That is why it is incumbent upon the communist Idea to respond to the question 'Where do correct ideas come from?' the way Mao did: 'correct ideas' (and by this I mean what constitutes the path of a truth in a situation) come from practice. 'Practice' should obviously be understood as the materialist name of the real. It would thus be appropriate to say that the Idea that symbolizes the becoming 'in truth' of correct (political) ideas in History, that is to say, the Idea of communism, therefore comes itself from the idea of practice (from the experience of the real) in the final analysis but can nevertheless not be reduced to it. This is because it is the protocol not of the existence but rather of the *exposure* of a truth in action.

All of the foregoing explains, and to a certain extent justifies, why it was ultimately possible to go to the extreme of exposing the truths of emancipatory politics in the guise of their opposite, that is to say, in the guise of a State. Since it is a question of an (imaginary) ideological relationship between a truth procedure and historical facts, why hesitate to push this relationship to its limit? Why not say that it is a matter of a relationship between event and State? *State and Revolution*: that is the title of one of Lenin's most famous texts. And the State and the Event are indeed what are at stake in it. Nevertheless, Lenin, following Marx in this regard, is careful to say that the State in question after the Revolution will have to be the State of the withering away of the State, the State as organizer of the transition to the non-State. So let's say the following: The Idea of communism can project the real of a politics, subtracted as ever from the power of the State, into the figure of 'another State', provided that the subtraction lies within this subjectivating operation, in the sense that the 'other State' is also subtracted from the power of the State, hence from its own power, in so far as it is a State whose essence is to wither away.

It is in this context that it is necessary to think and endorse the vital importance of proper names in all revolutionary politics. Their importance is indeed both spectacular and paradoxical. On the one hand, in effect, emancipatory politics is essentially the politics of the anonymous masses; it is the victory of those with no names,[10] of those who are held in a state of colossal

---

10   Those who have 'no name', those who have 'no part', and ultimately, in all current political actions, the organizing role of the workers 'without papers' are all part of a negative, or rather stripped down, view of the human terrain of emancipatory politics. Jacques Rancière, starting in particular with his in-depth study of these themes in the nineteenth century, has specifically highlighted, in the philosophical field, the implications for democracy of not belonging to a dominant societal category. This idea actually goes back at least as far as to the Marx of the *Manuscripts of 1844*, who defined the proletariat as generic humanity, since it does not itself possess any of the properties by which the bourgeoisie defines (respectable, or normal, or 'well-adjusted', as we would say today) Man. This idea is the basis of Rancière's attempt to salvage the word 'democracy', as is evident in his essay *The Hatred of Democracy* (Verso, 2006). I am not sure that the word can so easily be salvaged, or, at any rate, I think that making a detour through the Idea of communism is unavoidable. The debate has begun and will go on.

insignificance by the State. On the other hand, it is distinguished all along the way by proper names, which define it historically, which represent it, much more forcefully than is the case for other kinds of politics. Why is there this long series of proper names? Why this glorious Pantheon of revolutionary heroes? Why Spartacus, Thomas Müntzer, Robespierre, Toussaint Louverture, Blanqui, Marx, Lenin, Rosa Luxemburg, Mao, Che Guevara and so many others? The reason is that all these proper names symbolize historically – in the guise of an individual, of a pure singularity of body and thought – the rare and precious network of ephemeral sequences of politics as truth. The elusive formalism of bodies-of-truth is legible here as empirical existence. In these proper names, the ordinary individual discovers glorious, distinctive individuals as the mediation for his or her own individuality, as the proof that he or she can force its finitude. The anonymous action of millions of militants, rebels, fighters, unrepresentable as such, is combined and counted as one in the simple, powerful symbol of the proper name. Thus, proper names are involved in the operation of the Idea, and the ones I just mentioned are elements of the Idea of communism at its various different stages. So let us not hesitate to say that Khrushchev's condemnation of 'the cult of personality', apropos Stalin, was misguided, and that, under the pretence of democracy, it heralded the decline of the Idea of communism that we witnessed in the ensuing decades. The political critique of Stalin and his terrorist vision of the State needed to be undertaken in a rigorous way, from the perspective of revolutionary politics itself, and Mao had begun to do as much in a number of his writings.[11] Whereas Khrushchev, who was in fact defending the group that had led the Stalinist State, made no inroads whatsoever as regards this issue and, when it came to speaking of the Terror carried out under Stalin, merely offered an abstract critique of the role of proper names in political subjectivation. He himself thereby paved the way for the 'new philosophers' of reactionary humanism a decade later. Whence a very precious

---

11   Mao Zedong's writings on Stalin were published in the short book *Mao Tsé-Toung et la construction du socialisme*, clearly subtitled 'Modèle soviétique ou voie chinoise', translated and presented by Hu Chi-hsi (Seuil, 1975). Guided by the idea of the eternity of the True, I wrote a commentary on this book, in the preface to *Logics of Worlds*.

lesson: even though retroactive political actions may require that a given name be stripped of its symbolic function, this function as such cannot be eliminated for all that. For the Idea – and the communist Idea in particular, because it refers directly to the infinity of the people – needs the finitude of proper names.

Let's recapitulate as simply as possible. A truth is the political real. History, even as a reservoir of proper names, is a symbolic place. The ideological operation of the Idea of communism is the imaginary projection of the political real into the symbolic fiction of History, including in its guise as a representation of the action of innumerable masses via the One of a proper name. The role of this Idea is to support the individual's incorporation into the discipline of a truth procedure, to authorize the individual, in his or her own eyes, to go beyond the Statist constraints of mere survival by becoming a part of the body-of-truth, or the subjectivizable body.

We will now ask: why is it necessary to resort to this ambiguous operation? Why do the event and its consequences also have to be exposed in the guise of a fact – often a violent one – that is accompanied by different versions of the 'cult of personality'?

What is the reason for this historical appropriation of emancipatory politics?

The simplest reason is that ordinary history, the history of individual lives, is confined within the State. The history of a life, with neither decision nor choice, is in itself a part of the history of the State, whose conventional mediations are the family, work, the homeland, property, religion, customs and so forth. The heroic, but individual, projection of an exception to all the above – as is a truth procedure – also aims at being shared with everyone else; it aims to show itself to be not only an exception but also a possibility that everyone can share from now on. And that is one of the Idea's functions: to project the exception into the ordinary life of individuals, to fill what merely exists with a certain measure of the extraordinary. To convince my own immediate circle – husband or wife, neighbours and friends, colleagues – that the fantastic exception of truths in the making also exists, that we are not doomed to lives programmed by the constraints of the State. Naturally, in the final analysis, only the raw, or militant, experience of the truth procedure will compel one person or another's entry into the body-of-truth. But to take him or her to the place where

this experience is to be found – to make him or her a
spectator of, and therefore partly a participant in, what
is important for a truth – the mediation of the Idea,
the sharing of the Idea, are almost always required.
The Idea of communism (regardless of what name it
might otherwise be given, which hardly matters: no
Idea is definable by its name) is what enables a truth
procedure to be spoken in the impure language of the
State and thereby for the lines of force by virtue of
which the State prescribes what is possible and what
is impossible to be shifted for a time. In this view of
things, the most ordinary action is to take someone
to a real political meeting, far from their home, far
from their predetermined existential parameters, in
a hostel of workers from Mali, for example, or at the
gates of a factory. Once they have come to the place
where politics is occurring, they will make a decision
about whether to incorporate or withdraw. But in order
for them to come to that place, the Idea – and for two
centuries, or perhaps since Plato, it has been the Idea
of communism – must have already shifted them in the
order of representations, of History and of the State.
The symbol must imaginarily come to the aid of the
creative flight from the real. Allegorical facts must

ideologize and historicize the fragility of truth. A banal yet crucial discussion with four workers and a student in an ill-lit room must momentarily be enlarged to the dimensions of Communism and thus be both what it is and what it will have been as a moment in the local construction of the True. Through the enlargement of the symbol, it must become visible that 'just ideas' come from this practically invisible practice. The five-person meeting in an out-of-the-way suburb must be eternal in the very expression of its precariousness. That is why the real must be exposed in a fictional structure.

The second reason is that every event is a surprise. If this were not the case, it would mean that it would have been predictable as a fact, and so would be inscribed in the History of the State, which is a contradiction in terms. The problem can thus be formulated in the following way: how can we prepare ourselves for such surprises? And this time the problem really exists, even if we are already currently militants of a previous event's consequences, even if we are included in a body-of-truth. Granted, we are proposing the deployment of new possibilities. However, the event to come will turn what is still impossible, even for us, into a possibility.

In order to anticipate, at least ideologically, or
intellectually, the creation of new possibilities, we
must have an Idea. An Idea that of course involves the
newness of the possibilities that the truth procedure of
which we are the militants has brought to light, which
are real-possibilities, but an Idea that also involves
the formal possibility of *other* possibilities, ones as yet
unsuspected by us. An Idea is always the assertion
that a new truth is historically possible. And since
the forcing of the impossible into the possible occurs
via subtraction from the power of the State, an Idea
can be said to assert that this subtractive process is
infinite: it is always formally possible that the dividing
line drawn by the State between the possible and the
impossible may once again be shifted, however radical
its previous shifts – including the one in which we as
militants are currently taking part – may have been.
That is why one of the contents of the communist
Idea today – as opposed to the theme of communism
as a goal to be attained through the work of a new
State – is that the withering away of the State, while
undoubtedly a principle that must be apparent in any
political action (which is expressed by the formula
'politics at a distance from the State' as an obligatory

refusal of any direct inclusion in the State, of any request for funding from the State, of any participation in elections, etc.), is also an infinite task, since the creation of new political truths will always shift the dividing line between Statist, hence historical, facts and the eternal consequences of an event.

With this in mind, I will now conclude by turning to the contemporary inflections of the Idea of communism.[12] In keeping with the current reassessment of the Idea of communism, as I mentioned, the word's function can no longer be that of an adjective, as in 'Communist Party', or 'communist regimes'. The Party-form, like that of the Socialist State, is no longer suitable for providing real support for the Idea. This problem moreover first found negative expression in two crucial events of the '60s and '70s of the last century: the Cultural Revolution in China and the amorphous entity called 'May '68' in France. Later, new political

---

12 On the three stages of the Idea of communism, especially the one (the second stage) during which the Idea of communism attempted to be overtly political (in the sense of the programme, of both the Party and the State), see the final chapters of my *Circonstances 4*, published in English as *The Meaning of Sarkozy* (Verso, 2008).

forms, all of which are of the order of politics without a party, were – and are still being – tried out.[13] Overall, however, the modern, so-called 'democratic' form of the bourgeois State, of which globalized capitalism is the cornerstone, can boast of having no rivals in the ideological field. For three decades now, the word 'communism' has been either totally forgotten or practically equated with criminal enterprises. That is why the subjective situation of politics has everywhere become so incoherent. Lacking the Idea, the popular masses's confusion is inescapable.

Nevertheless, there are many signs suggesting that this reactionary period is coming to an end. The historical paradox is that, in a certain way, we are closer to problems investigated in the first half of the nineteenth century than we are to those we have inherited from the twentieth. Just as in around 1840,

---

13   There have been numerous, fascinating experiments with new political forms over the past three decades. The following could be mentioned: the Solidarity movement in Poland in 1980–81; the first sequence of the Iranian Revolution; the *Organisation Politique* in France; the Zapatista movement in Mexico; the Maoists in Nepal . . . This list is not intended to be exhaustive.

today we are faced with an utterly cynical capitalism, which is certain that it is the only possible option for a rational organization of society. Everywhere it is implied that the poor are to blame for their own plight, that Africans are backward, and that the future belongs either to the 'civilized' bourgeoisies of the Western world or to those who, like the Japanese, choose to follow the same path. Today, just as back then, very extensive areas of extreme poverty can be found even in the rich countries. There are outrageous, widening inequalities between countries, as well as between social classes. The subjective, political gulf between Third World farmers, the unemployed and poor wage earners in our so-called 'developed' countries, on the one hand, and the 'Western' middle classes on the other, is absolutely unbridgeable and tainted with a sort of indifference bordering on hatred. More than ever, political power, as the current economic crisis with its one single slogan of 'rescue the banks' clearly proves, is merely an agent of capitalism. Revolutionaries are divided and only weakly organized, broad sectors of working-class youth have fallen prey to nihilistic despair, the vast majority of intellectuals are servile. In contrast to all this, as isolated as Marx and his friends were at the time when the retrospectively famous *Manifesto of the Communist Party* came out in 1847, there are nonetheless more and more of us involved in organizing new types of political processes among the poor and working masses and in trying to find every possible way to support the re-emergent forms of the communist Idea in reality. Just as at the beginning of the nineteenth century, the victory of the communist Idea is not at issue, as it would later be, far too dangerously and dogmatically, for a whole stretch of the twentieth century. What matters first and foremost is its existence and the terms in which it is formulated. In the first place, to provide a vigorous subjective existence to the communist hypothesis is the task those of us gathered here today are attempting to accomplish in our own way. And it is, I insist, a thrilling task. By combining intellectual constructs, which are always global and universal, with experiments of fragments of truths, which are local and singular, yet universally transmittable, we can give new life to the communist hypothesis, or rather to the Idea of communism, in individual consciousnesses. We can usher in the third era of this Idea's existence. We can, so we must.

Appendix

Letter from Alain Badiou to Slavoj Žižek: On the Work of Mao Zedong

Dear Slavoj,

Your introduction to the Verso edition of Mao's philosophical-political texts is, as always, of very great interest.[1] Let me begin by refuting, as I usually do, your reputation as a showman and a conceptual poseur – a very French misrepresentation (but let's not worry that they said the same about our master Lacan) – and by saying that your introduction is honest, profound and brave. It is honest because there is no showiness or vague rhetoric; this is an accurate expression of your very ambivalent relationship with the figure of Mao. You recognize the novelty and breadth of his vision but take the view that it is, in many essential

---

1 See Žižek's introduction to Mao Zedong, *On Practice and Contradiction*, Verso, 2007. *Translator's note.*

respects, false and dangerous. It is profound because you cut straight to the crucial and difficult question of the relationship between contemporary dialectical thought and politics. Your comments on the negation of the negation are remarkable. You explain, probably for the first time, the underlying reasons why Stalin and Mao reject that 'law'. They fail, that is, to understand its real Hegelian meaning: *any immanent negation is, in its essence, a negation of the negation that it is.* Your text is, finally brave because, as so often, you lay yourself open to criticism from both sides. The counter-revolutionary descendants of our 'new philosophers' will scream, as they are already doing, that you and Badiou are both backward-looking, but still dangerous, supporters of a sepulchral communism. What else could the simple fact of talking about Mao mean to this new generation of watchdogs? Even so, those who remain true to what was, in the lineage of Mao, known in Europe as 'Maoism' – and I am probably now one of its few noteworthy representatives – will have some criticisms to make. You are familiar with this kind of 'struggle on both fronts', which was a basic slogan of the Cultural Revolution: the struggle against the classic bourgeoisie, whose epicentre is American imperialism, and against the new bureaucratic bourgeoisie whose epicentre was at the time the Soviet Union.

Speaking of the existence of this new bourgeoisie in China, Mao used to say that, in a socialist country, the bourgeoisie was to be found 'right inside the Communist Party'. Given what Deng Xiaoping's 'reforms' have done to China, it really can be said that his words were prophetic. It can also be said that they illustrate the extent to which Mao created *a new politics of the negation of the negation*, despite his own comments and your own commentaries, which are quite justified. The *new negation* of this process does indeed take place in the very heart of the Party, which is the acknowledged leader of the process of the destruction of the old world. That negation is now consensual: 'bourgeoisie', and even more so 'new bourgeoisie', are terms that have been banished from all official discourses of both the majority and the opposition.

This brings us to a vital methodological point and there is, I think, no disagreement of principle between us here. When it comes to figures like Robespierre, Saint-Just, Babeuf, Blanqui, Bakunin, Marx, Engels,

Lenin, Stalin, Mao Zedong, Zhou Enlai, Tito, Enver Hoxha, Guevara, Castro and a few others (I am thinking of Aristide in particular), it is vital not to give any ground in the context of criminalization and hair-raising anecdotes in which the forces of reaction have always tried to wall them up and invalidate them. We can and must discuss amongst ourselves (meaning those for whom capitalism and its political forms are horrors, and for whom egalitarian emancipation is the only maxim that has any universal value) the use we make, or do not make, of these figures. The discussion may be lively, and sometimes antagonistic, but it is amongst ourselves, and the rules of the discussion imply an absolute refusal to collaborate with the adversary's ranting. Even the establishment of the facts and historical rigour must be completely on our side. Any new book about Mao, whether officially authorized or 'neutral', and any sensational 'biography', is obviously a piece of propaganda, completely mendacious, perfidious and devoid of all interest. You cite the book by Jung Chang and Jon Halliday, which is a typical product of the genre. Bush himself, who was famous for not reading anything, avidly read, he says, a biography of

Mao and learned, to his great and pathetic amazement, that Mao personally killed seventy million people, which indubitably makes him the biggest *serial killer* in history.

It seems to me that, when it comes to the details, you do not always get away from the image of the last great Marxist revolutionary in world history – an idea that is at once nonsensical and repellent – that our dear West propagates, and which is in fact promoted or even manipulated by the Chinese State (which is, let us remember, in the hands of those who are bent on taking revenge for the Cultural Revolution, and who have become the corrupt lords of capitalist accumulation). On the one hand, you stray too far from the extremely tense context of the international politics of the day. One cannot, for example, speak of the famous exchange of 'food for guns' that supposedly reduced China to starvation in the 1950s to the benefit of the USSR without recalling that, from 1950 onwards, the Chinese army was waging a full-scale war against the Americans in Korea, and that it then offered a safe haven for the Vietnamese during their 20-year war of national liberation. And nor can one speak of the experiments in mass production and the

industrialization of the countryside, including the
'Great Leap Forward', without evoking the split, at first
latent and then explicit, with the Soviet Godfather. The
split was a political necessity, and there is no denying
that it was a revolutionary duty, but it did expose
China to enormous dangers. The Godfather's economic
retaliation was unprecedentedly swift and forced the
Chinese communists to envisage a protracted period of
autarchy at the very time when they still had to prepare
for war. The attempt to be 'self-reliant' (a vital Maoist
principle) and to develop the productive forces by all
means possible was, for an isolated country that was
being simultaneously provoked by both superpowers,
a question of survival.

I also think that you find some of the 'cultural'
aspects of Mao's style (such as his 'cosmological'
vision, which is, in my view, nothing more than a
set of metaphors) amusing or even fascinating, while
others leave you cold. You do not, for instance, always
understand the 'peasant-style' Chinese humour that
characterizes many of Mao's interventions (even
when, joking about the number of dead, he reminds
us: 'Once a head is chopped off . . . it can't be
restored, nor can it grow back again as chives do

after being cut'[2]). The other problem is that, because your own sense of humour tends to be on the black side because it comes from the East, and because of your in-depth knowledge of the mysteries of the Stalinist regime, you are too quick to project its macabre parameters on to what is in fact the very different world of communist China. Do I have to remind you that, with the notable exception of Liu Shao Si, and probably Lin Piao, none of Mao's sworn enemies in the Party leadership lost their lives, even when the violence of the Cultural Revolution was at its height? And that almost all of them regained their positions and their power from the mid-'70s onwards? In the long term, Deng Xiaoping, who was vilified, denounced and caricatured as 'the number two person in authority taking the capitalist road' – and quite rightly so, as the future was to demonstrate – became the country's new master. What a difference from Stalin, who was obsessed with exterminating the Bolshevik 'old guard'! That in itself reveals the huge

---

2 'On The Ten Major Relationships', *Selected Works of Mao Tse-Tung Vol. V*, pp. 299–300, Foreign Languages Press, 1977. *Translator's note*.

difference between the Cultural Revolution and the Soviet purges of the 1930s, no matter what you say to the contrary.

That, however, is not the important point. What I would like to get across to you above all else is that your definitions of the points that might raise the issue of the universality of Mao are not sufficiently rigorous. Were it not for that universality, both the publication of these texts and our commentaries – both yours and mine – would not be of the slightest interest.

Indeed, one corollary of the radical precautionary principle we have to observe in the face of the never-ending flood of counter-revolutionary propaganda, is that we must never leave the problematic field of the politics of emancipation (otherwise known as communist politics) within which we read, value or criticise the works of Mao. And, as is always the case when we are dealing with what I call 'truth procedures', that field is constructed on the basis of problems. It is a question of dealing with problems, suggesting theoretical and practical solutions, making mistakes and correcting them and bequeathing the results to those whom Mao, being very worried about this question, called 'Successors for the revolutionary cause'.[3] A few principles, a few resolved problems and a few new problems to which there is no known solution: that is why the work of the revolutionary leaders of the past is of such importance to us, and when we talk amongst ourselves, we should not be talking of anything else.

The first question must therefore be: what problems do we and Mao still have in common? In what sense is a reading of his texts anything more than an exercise in nostalgia or critique? To what extent can Mao's texts still be a point of reference in our search for a new direction for emancipatory politics, in the sense that certain of Poincaré's memoirs on the theory of dynamic systems are still a source of inspiration for mathematicians?

If we are to go into this question in any real sense, we must first establish our starting point, namely the period between 1925 and 1955, when Stalin's vision was hegemonic throughout the international communist movement. It has to be remembered that its hegemony was based upon an unprecedented

---

3 *Quotations From Chairman Mao Tse-Tung*, Foreign Languages Press, 1967, p. 276. *Translator's note.*

event: the first victorious people's revolution in Russia in October 1917. And we must constantly bear in mind that this victory – which was revenge for the workers' insurrections crushed during the nineteenth century, including that in France – was universally attributed to the new political discipline embodied in the Leninist-style Party. As a result, everything that came after it, including the anti-Stalinist Trotskyists, was defined and shaped by the question of the class Party or the workers' organization, if you wish to put it that way. We can therefore put it in a nutshell: the universality of Mao, assuming that it does exist, has to do with the new solutions to and/or the identification of new problems of Leninism, and therefore with the link between the political process and the Party.

Many aspects of Mao's thought are, of course, innovative, and you mention almost all of them: the importance of the peasantry, which is so often disparaged in the name of workerist fetishism; protracted people's war, which is essential when a short-term urban insurrection is not possible; the exceptional importance accorded to ideology and political subjectivity; the theory that there is a 'new bourgeoisie' inside the Communist Party and that the best way of fighting it is to rely upon the mass movement, and even the spontaneity of the masses, and not the political police or institutionalized purges; the distinction between different types of contradiction, and their immanent fluidity, and so on. But none of this could constitute a political truth in itself, had not all these themes been ultimately articulated with the central problem of the Party, defined by Stalin as the sole source of and sole actor in the process known as the 'building of socialism'. If we fail to relate the special features of Maoism to this problem, which is in a sense *the* revolutionary problem of the period, we lapse into a defensive empiricism that makes too many concessions to the enemies of all egalitarian revolutions.

We can in fact find in Mao's earliest writings, which seem to be classically Stalinist ('Without its Communist Party, the people has nothing'), some curious reservations about anything that might give the Party a monopoly on the leadership of the popular political process. In *Logics of Worlds*, I make a very close analysis of this point in the work of the young Mao, which was written at the start of the people's war in the Chingkang mountains in 1927. According to Mao, 'red political power' is made up of differentiated elements, and the people's assemblies are as important as the Party itself. And besides, it was the question of the Army that was decisive at this stage. Now, while it is true that 'the party commands the gun', it is also true that 'without a people's army, the people has nothing', and that formula is a counter-balance to Stalin's. Indeed, 'The Chinese Red Army is an armed body for carrying out the political tasks of the revolution',[4] which implies that the Party has no monopoly on those tasks. Forty years later, during the Cultural Revolution, we will once more see 'revolutionary committees' and the Red Army attempting to check the all-powerful Party's monolithic hold over relations between the mass movement and the State.

Even Mao's dialectical thought helps to relativize the powers of the Party. For his maxim is not 'No communism without the Communist Party', but 'in order to have communism there must be a Communist Party'. This means that the Party, which is the leading organ of the State and the main agency in the building

---

4   Ibid., p. 100. *Translator's note.*

of socialism, derives its legitimacy only from as complete an exposition as possible of the way *it* is negated by the action of the masses who rebel against it. The famous formula 'It is right to rebel against reactionaries' obviously means: 'It is right to rebel against the ossified form of negation embodied in the bureaucracy of the Party-State.'

It is in this context that we must accept that there was an element of universality in the terrible failure of the Cultural Revolution. And let us remember in this context that the fact that something ends in bloody failure is not the only thing that can be said of it. Once again, you use the failure of the Cultural Revolution as a facile argument in order to deny its importance and contemporary relevance (and let us remember that Mao argued that it would take another 10 or 20 revolutions to push society in the direction of communism). Everyone knows that Lenin's thought is grounded in his opinion of the Paris Commune, even though the workers' revolt ended with an unprecedented massacre. Marx had already formulated the political problem raised by the Commune: given that the working class had the political ability to seize State power (and the Communards held power

in Paris for over two months), how can we ensure that
the seizure of power can, first, be extended in spatial
terms and, second, that it can last in temporal terms?
His provisional answer, which is still too general, is
that we cannot be content with *seizing* State power as
such and must *destroy* the machine of the bourgeois
State. Lenin forged the real historical answer to the
problem bequeathed us by the Commune in the
form of a centralized Party with 'iron discipline'. He
created the instrument – and although it is a political
instrument, Lenin's model is a military machine –
that could bring about the 'destruction' Marx wanted,
and that could replace the bourgeois State with a new
kind of State exercising a popular despotism without
historical precedent: the State of the dictatorship of
the proletariat, which is in fact a State that merges
with the insurrectional Party and which, to a large
extent, militarizes the whole of society. The Stalinist
terror was a post-insurrectional way of using a tool that
was designed to ensure the victory of an insurrection:
an internal political problem was handled as though it
were a problem of the military type, and that implied
the physical destruction of the enemy, or so-called
enemy.

We can now describe the problem that Mao and the millions of militants who, between 1966 and 1976, acted in his name in China and the rest of the world tried to resolve. The Cultural Revolution was described by Mao as the final realization of the principles of the Paris Commune. What does that mean? For Mao, it meant that, even though the official position of the Chinese communists, who opposed Khrushchev and his successors, seemed to be saying the opposite, we have to conclude that, on the whole, the balance sheet of Stalin was negative. Why? Because, Mao tells us, Stalin was interested in the cadres and never the masses. As we know, Stalin held that 'When the line has been established, cadres decide everything.' According to Mao, 'The people, and the people alone, are the active force in the making of world history . . . While we [communists] are often childish and ignorant.'[5] We must therefore ensure as a matter of urgency that the political process that leads to communism – and therefore the 'dictatorship of the proletariat' – rediscovers its sources and its basic actors in popular mass uprisings, as it did in

---

5   Ibid., p. 118. *Translator's note.*

1927, and not in the Party apparatchiks. The forces available for this trial of strength were, first, educated youth (mobilized all over the world in the 1960s), the youngest and most politicized fraction of the workers, and some detachments of the Red Army. It was to these forces that Mao and those close to him turned from 1966 onwards. They plunged China into chaos for ten years, but launched ideas, slogans, organizational forms and theoretical schemas whose power has yet to be exhausted.

The failure of this extraordinary uprising, whose freedom – reflected in hundreds of new organizations, thousands of newspapers, giant posters, constant meetings and countless clashes – is still astonishing, was no more due to the nature of the problem it was trying to resolve than the failure of the Paris Commune was due to the fact that the workers rose up in rebellion, which was quite natural and necessary in the circumstances that were forced upon them. It was due to the fact that the movement could not dialectically interact at the national level with forms of organization that could have really modified the schema of the Party-State. As throughout the Paris Commune, the absence of any effective centralized leadership (a real Party) led to anarchic divisions and impotence. In China, a myriad of factions undermined a form of collective action. The most advanced form of local organization, which, significantly enough, adopted the name 'the Shanghai Commune' at the beginning of 1967, did not succeed in becoming a national paradigm and finally collapsed, leaving the field open to the Party's *revanchards*.

Basically, the *problem* was very real (how to take the political process of communism beyond State action and into the life of the people). The *attempt* to do so taught us some universal lessons (there must be a direct alliance between intellectual youth and the workers; we have to experiment with non-party forms of organization; education must undergo a metamorphosis; the division of labour must be destroyed; power in the factories must be reorganized along democratic lines; new links must be established between town and countryside; we must create a new and popular intellectuality, and so on). The *failure* to do so means that we must abandon once and for all the militarized paradigm of the Party, and move towards what the *Organisation politique* in France calls a 'politics without parties'. We have now reached that point, and we have reached it because the Cultural Revolution brought us here.

We can therefore say without fear that, in the current phase of revolutionary politics, the Cultural Revolution plays the role that the Paris Commune played in its Leninist sequence. *The Cultural Revolution is the Commune of the age of Communist Parties and Socialist States: a terrible failure that teaches us some essential lessons.*

I will end by saying that the direct link you think you can establish between the Cultural Revolution and the furious capitalist accumulation that is now ravaging China is just window-dressing. One could just as easily say that the failure of the Paris Commune in France led directly, at the end of the nineteenth century, to a long period of imperialist expansion and unfettered political wheeling and dealing that finally led to the slaughter of 1914–18. Obvious, isn't it? When a grandiose attempt to resolve a political problem of the day is made by revolutionaries and ends in failure, the enemy is going to be firmly in the saddle for quite a while! But Delescluze, Vallès, Louise Michel, Varlin and Blanqui were no more responsible for the colonialism and corruption of the *belle époque* than Mao and his comrades are responsible for the China of the billionaires in Shanghai or for globalized corruption. The true descendants of the Communards are Lenin, Rosa Luxemburg and all the other revolutionaries who overcame the aporiae of the Commune, but still took it as a starting point. And their descendants are trying to find their way and experiment with ways to deal with the problem bequeathed them by the Cultural Revolution: that of a political process 'without a party', but which still takes as its starting point the universal aspects of that attempt to resolve it. I think that we are both their descendants. Which is why a certain Yves-Charles Zarka, who writes for *Le Figaro*, is not mistaken when, in a hyperbolic eulogy, he identifies both of us as 'philosophers of Terror'.[6]

Yours in friendship, my dear Slavoj.

---

6   Yves-Charles Zarka, 'Badiou, Žižek, le retour de la Terreur', *Le Figaro*, 27 March 2008. *Translator's note*.